MW00772855

TO

....

FROM

....

ON THIS DATE

....

Jean Fischer

BIBLE MEMORY

Plan & Devotional

for Women

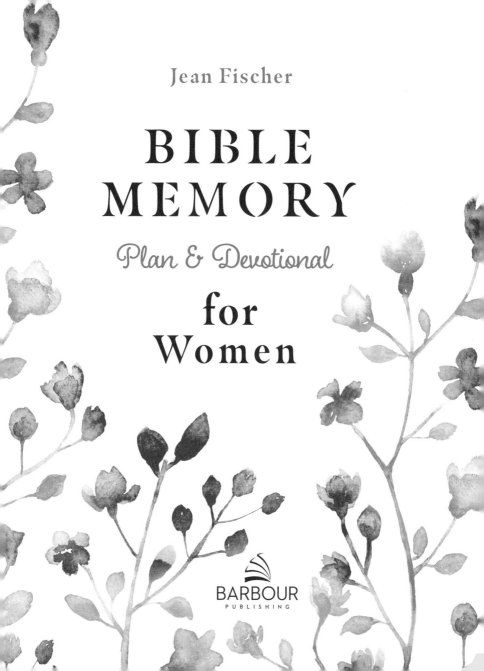

BARBOUR
PUBLISHING

Cover Design: Greg Jackson, Thinkpen Design

Published by Barbour Publishing, Inc., 1810 Barbour Drive, Uhrichsville, Ohio 44683, www.barbourbooks.com

Our mission is to inspire the world with the life-changing message of the Bible.

Member of the
Evangelical Christian
Publishers Association

Printed in China.

CONTENTS

INTRODUCTION

What would you give to know the secrets to receiving comfort and strength, making wise decisions, forgiving yourself and others, and finding true love? With a little time and commitment, you can unlock these secrets and more by studying the Bible.

The Bible is like a key. Studying God's Word brings you nearer to Him. It unlocks His answers to your questions and His plans for your life. When you store God's words in your heart, they remain there ready to help you in any circumstance.

The *Bible Memory Plan and Devotional for Women* helps you memorize God's Word as it leads you through topics like worry, patience, friendship, marriage, and love. Each entry begins with a scripture verse and a devotion about that scripture. Then, following each reading, you will find encouragement and tips for memorizing several scripture verses.

Memorizing God's Word allows you to put scripture into action. Whenever you have a need, you can recall His words, and God will meet you wherever you are—in the laundry room, while driving your kids to soccer practice, at work, or at play. With scripture in your heart, you will hear God speaking to you, encouraging you, comforting you, and leading you according to His will.

Proverbs 7:2–3 (TLB) says, "Guard my words as your most precious possession. Write them down, and also keep them deep within your heart." The *Bible Memory Plan and Devotional for Women* will help you to do that. So let's get started.

SURRENDER

*If you try to save your life,
you will lose it. But if you give it
up for me, you will surely find it.*

MATTHEW 10:39 CEV

Judson Van DeVenter struggled with a decision. Should he follow his dream to become a famous artist or give it up to become a minister? He wavered for five years, never at peace and wondering what to do. Then, at a church revival it became clear. Van DeVenter surrendered his decision to God. "It was then that a new day was ushered into my life," he said.

God's plan sent him into active Christian service and in a way that he had not imagined. In his own words: "God had hidden a song in my heart, and touching a tender chord, He caused me to sing." His new God-given talent led Van DeVenter to write the well-known hymn "I Surrender All."

Practice surrendering your decisions to God. Surrender leads to a peaceful heart in alignment with His will.

Write God's Word on Your Heart Today

The apostle Paul said, "With thankful hearts, sing psalms, hymns, and spiritual songs to God" (Colossians 3:16 CEV). You might choose to include Judson Van DeVenter's song "I Surrender All" in your worship time today. If you are not familiar with the melody, you can find it through an online search. Sing the first verse and refrain.

> All to Jesus I surrender;
> All to Him I freely give;
> I will ever love and trust Him,
> In His presence daily live.
>
> Refrain:
> I surrender all,
> I surrender all;
> All to Thee, my blessed Savior,
> I surrender all.
>
> —Judson W. Van DeVenter, 1896

It takes work to surrender all aspects of your life to God, but when you learn to allow Him to control your heart, He will lead you into a brand-new day, just as He did Judson Van DeVenter. Practice surrender by memorizing these two verses and repeating them every morning:

With all your heart you must trust the Lord and not your own judgment. Always let him lead you, and he will clear the road for you to follow.
Proverbs 3:5–6 cev

Be still before the Lord and wait patiently for him.
Psalm 37:7 niv

End with this prayer:

Dear God, help me to surrender every part of my life to You. Fill my heart with Your presence and lead me according to Your will. Amen.

FAITH

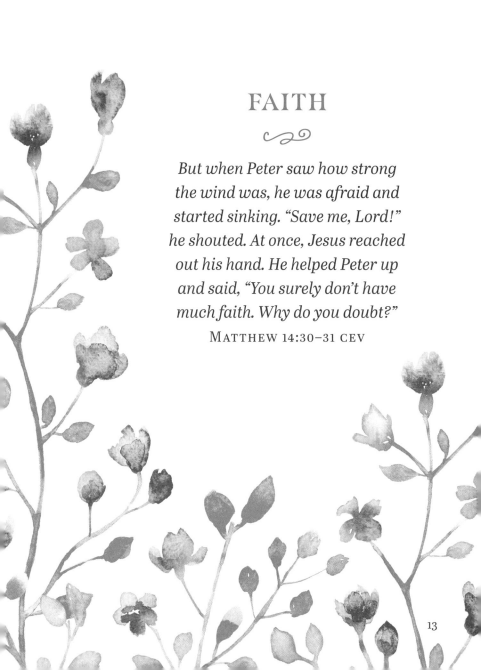

But when Peter saw how strong the wind was, he was afraid and started sinking. "Save me, Lord!" he shouted. At once, Jesus reached out his hand. He helped Peter up and said, "You surely don't have much faith. Why do you doubt?"

MATTHEW 14:30–31 CEV

Are you a perfect wife, mother, daughter, or friend? Are you perfect at whatever you set out to do? Perfection is impossible. No one is perfect except God, and He is able to perfectly handle whatever you entrust to Him.

Instead of working hard at being perfect, work harder at building your faith. Faith is the foundation on which you build hope. With faith, you say to God, "I believe that all things are possible through You." Stand on your faith and allow God to work. All He asks is that you try. If you doubt and begin to sink like Peter did, be assured that God is ready to take your hand and help you get up.

Write God's Word on Your Heart Today

Think about the little things in life that you accept by faith: that an order you placed will be ready when you arrive to pick it up or that your car will start tomorrow morning. If you have faith in these everyday things, then surely you can have faith in God.

The Bible defines faith as "confidence in what we hope for and assurance about what we do not see" (Hebrews 11:1 NIV). Faith begins by believing that God is real, that He is good, and that He wants His best for us. The Bible teaches in Hebrews 11:6 (NIV), "Without faith it is impossible to please God, because anyone who comes to him must believe that he exists and that he rewards those who earnestly seek him."

Can you name people from the Bible who acted by faith? Read about God's most faithful followers in Hebrews 11:4–39.

A powerful element of faith is trusting in God's Word. Write the following verses on index cards, commit them to memory,

and rely on them whenever your faith wears thin.

So we fix our eyes not on what is seen,
but on what is unseen, since what is seen is
temporary, but what is unseen is eternal.

2 Corinthians 4:18 niv

"Blessed are those who believe without seeing me."

John 20:29 nlt

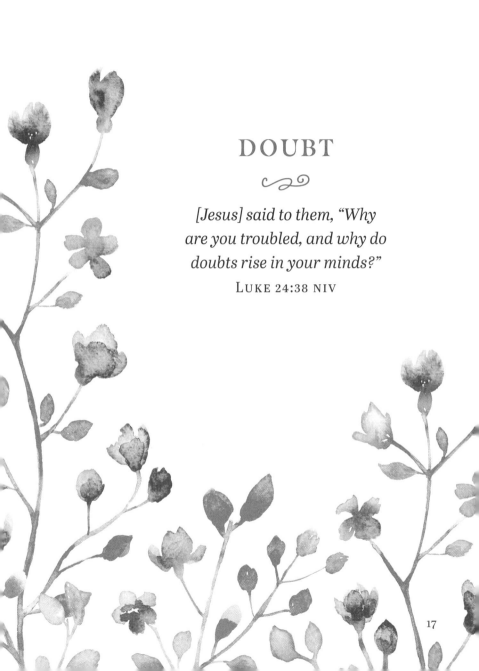

DOUBT

*[Jesus] said to them, "Why
are you troubled, and why do
doubts rise in your minds?"*

LUKE 24:38 NIV

As Jennifer's wedding approached, stress overwhelmed her—stress with a healthy dose of doubt. "I doubt that everything will be done on time!" she said. Between the cake, the caterer, the hall, and the decorations, all the deadlines made Jennifer wonder why she hadn't planned to elope.

Satan enjoys infusing the best-laid plans with doubt. Even on that most joyous occasion when Jesus rose from the grave, doubt seized His disciples. Had it really happened? Was Jesus alive? Satan planted a seed of doubt, hoping that it would grow inside their hearts. But Jesus knew better. He was well aware that humans are prone to doubt. So He showed up where His disciples had gathered and proved to them that it was He.

When worry and doubt fill your mind, you can count on this: Jesus will show up. He is real and willing to help you. Trust Him completely, and watch the doubt melt away.

Write God's Word on Your Heart Today

Some people doubt everything about God, from His very existence to His ability to do absolutely anything. Nothing is beyond God's power, but still they doubt. Doubt has teased humans from the beginning. When studying the Bible, we learn that Sarah and Abraham laughed at God's promise to give them a child. Gideon tested God by asking Him to perform a series of miracles to prove that He was real. Even Thomas, Jesus' faithful disciple, doubted the resurrection until he had touched the wound in his Savior's side. Doubt lurks nearby at work, home, and play. But you can be ready by memorizing these Bible verses and repeating them to yourself throughout the day.

When you get up in the morning:

I can do all things through Christ,
because he gives me strength.

PHILIPPIANS 4:13 NCV

During the day:

> *Show me your ways, Lord, teach me your paths.*
> *Guide me in your truth and teach me, for you are*
> *God my Savior, and my hope is in you all day long.*
>
> PSALM 25:4–5 NIV

At night:

> *"I do believe; help me overcome my unbelief!"*
>
> MARK 9:24 NIV

We are capable only within our ability as humans to believe completely and without doubt, and because we are not perfect, doubt will sometimes come into our thoughts. When you ask Jesus to help with your unbelief, He will reward you with faith.

TRUST

*It is better to take refuge in the
L*ORD *than to trust in humans.*

PSALM 118:8 NIV

Trust-building exercises are everywhere. Businesses use them to help their employees work together trusting one another. Maybe you have seen the exercise in which a person, eyes closed, falls backward, trusting her partners to catch her. Of course she knows that they will, but still there is an element of fear. *What if?*

Human trust is limited. David writes in Psalm 146:3–4 (CEV), "You can't depend on anyone, not even a great leader. Once they die and are buried, that will be the end of all their plans." This is why trust in God is so important. Humans are human. Life sometimes gets in the way of trust, and things change.

God is the only one who is always 100 percent trustworthy. He never changes. You can count on Him to be completely focused on you all the time, and He will never let you fall.

Write God's Word on Your Heart Today

Meditating on the general idea of a scripture verse can help you commit it to memory. Take the essence of a verse and make it personal. For example, before attempting to memorize the following verse, think about the places where you feel most safe. God is in all those places. You can trust Him to be wherever you are.

I will say of the Lord, "He is my refuge and my fortress, my God, in whom I trust."
PSALM 91:2 NIV

Now, think about people whom you trust for protection: your spouse and other family members, close friends, police officers. Why do you trust them? God is more trustworthy than any person. Wherever you go, He is your bodyguard, your protector. Memorize this verse:

The Lord is good, giving protection in times of trouble. He knows who trusts in him.
NAHUM 1:7 NCV

Finally, think about how it would feel to experience perfect peace. What if you could trust someone completely to handle every problem, to solve all disagreements, to know exactly what you should do in any situation? That person is God. Memorize this verse to remind you that He is infinitely trustworthy and that trusting Him gives you peace:

> *You, LORD, give true peace to those who*
> *depend on you, because they trust you.*
> ISAIAH 26:3 NCV

WORRY

*"Therefore do not worry about
tomorrow, for tomorrow
will worry about itself."*

MATTHEW 6:34 NIV

How often have you chased after your child, taken her hand, and told her to wait? Children want to know what lies ahead, and parents know the importance of keeping them in their sight. Parents understand that the world is a dangerous place, and they worry—"What if you had run into the street and been hit? What if you had gotten lost?"

Of course awareness and caution are necessary, but worry is when our thoughts run on ahead of God. Worry focuses on perceived trouble instead of the firm grip that God has on your hand. *What if things don't work out the way I want them to? What if I don't have enough money? What if I get sick?* Whatever you worry about, you have a heavenly Father who already knows what is around the next corner and always has you in His sight. He knows what to do, and He will take care of you.

Write God's Word on Your Heart Today

Worry is normal. Everyone worries. But worry is contrary to God's commands. Read what Jesus says about worry in Matthew 6:25–34. Worry is like thinking we are greater than God, the one who controls everything. In Psalm 55:22 (NCV), David provides these instructions: "Give your worries to the Lord, and he will take care of you. He will never let good people down."

One way to offset worry is to memorize and act on this verse from the apostle Paul: "Keep your minds on whatever is true, pure, right, holy, friendly, and proper. Don't ever stop thinking about what is truly worthwhile and worthy of praise" (Philippians 4:8 CEV).

Notice that this verse is in the present tense. Keep your minds on what *is* rather than what might be. To help you memorize the verse, write it on a chalkboard or dry-erase board set in your office, kitchen, or wherever you spend time. Practice listing, in order, the following eight elements—the kinds of thoughts that offset worry. Then incorporate them into the verse.

27

1. True
2. Pure
3. Right
4. Holy
5. Friendly
6. Proper
7. Worthwhile
8. Worthy

Sometimes, you will need more than Paul's list. When worrisome thoughts bother you, try stopping them by memorizing and repeating this verse:

Be still, and know that I am God.

PSALM 46:10 KJV

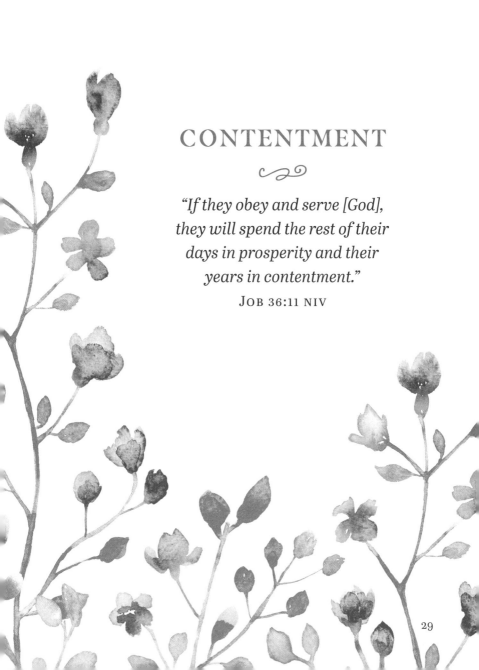

CONTENTMENT

*"If they obey and serve [God],
they will spend the rest of their
days in prosperity and their
years in contentment."*

JOB 36:11 NIV

The book of Philippians is a letter Paul wrote while imprisoned in Rome. In Philippians 4:11–12 (NIV) he writes: "I have learned to be content whatever the circumstances. I know what it is to be in need, and I know what it is to have plenty. I have learned the secret of being content in any and every situation, whether well fed or hungry, whether living in plenty or in want."

Imagine finding contentment while chained to a wall in a stone-cold prison. But that is exactly what Paul did; he found the secret to contentment. And he shared that secret in verse 13— "I can do all this through him who gives me strength" (NIV).

You can find contentment too. Put your faith in Jesus. Allow Him to be your everything and find comfort in His love.

Write God's Word on Your Heart Today

When Paul wrote, "I can do all this through him who gives me strength," he was telling about Christ's love. When you surrender your heart to Christ and trust in His love, He gives you strength to carry out His perfect will.

When memorizing scripture, it helps to concentrate on its nouns—words like *Christ* and *strength*.

Focus on the word *love* in the following memory verse:

> *Your love means more than*
> *life to me, and I praise you.*
> PSALM 63:3 CEV

Create a picture in your mind, something that represents love, perhaps a heart. Now, add to that image Christ presenting you with the heart and you on your knees praising Him. Allow that picture to help while you memorize the verse. You can use similar mental pictures to memorize almost any passage of scripture.

David was another man who found the secret to contentment. He found it in humility and by turning his worries over to God. In Psalm 131, David wrote: "But I have calmed and quieted myself, I am like a weaned child with its mother; like a weaned child I am content" (Psalm 131:2 NIV). Choose a noun to focus on in this verse. Then create a picture in your mind to help you memorize it. Perhaps you like to draw. You might even try sketching the image while you memorize the verse.

HOPE

*"But blessed are those who trust
in the LORD and have made the
LORD their hope and confidence."*

JEREMIAH 17:7 NLT

The Gospels of Matthew, Mark, and Luke tell the story of a woman with a blood issue. There is little said about her, only that she suffered from bleeding for twelve years. She hoped for a cure and spent all her money on doctors and remedies. None of them worked. Then, she heard about Jesus, the Healer. She was considered unclean because of her problem. According to Jewish law, anyone she touched would be made unclean. So she took an enormous risk pushing her way through the great crowd surrounding Jesus. She hoped that just by touching His robe she would be healed. Jesus felt her fingers brush against Him. In the middle of the crowd pushing in on Him, He felt her hope, and He healed her "straightaway," or immediately, as Mark tells us.

Is Jesus your hope for a transformed life, a better future? When all else fails, there is always hope in Him.

Write God's Word on Your Heart Today

David is perhaps the most well-known person of the Old Testament. Much is written about him—how he rose above the abuse shown him by his elder brothers, his bravery against the giant Goliath, his friendship with King Saul's son, Jonathan, and Saul's jealousy toward him. David overcame many hardships and became Israel's greatest king. He was also a talented musician who wrote hymns and prayers called psalms.

Today's memory verses are about hope from the psalms of David:

You are my refuge and my shield;
I have put my hope in your word.

PSALM 119:114 NIV

You answer us with awesome and righteous
deeds, God our Savior, the hope of all the ends
of the earth and of the farthest seas.

PSALM 65:5 NIV

Guide me in your truth and teach me, for you are
God my Savior, and my hope is in you all day long.

As a tool to help you memorize these verses, try incorporating them into a prayer:

Dear God, You are my refuge and my shield; I have put
my hope in Your Word. You answer us with awesome
and righteous deeds, God our Savior, the hope of all
the ends of the earth and of the farthest seas. Guide
me in Your truth and teach me, for You are God my
Savior, and my hope is in You all day long. Amen.

Make this prayer of hope a part of your daily prayer and worship.

GRACE

*Let us then approach God's throne
of grace with confidence, so that we
may receive mercy and find grace
to help us in our time of need.*

HEBREWS 4:16 NIV

Grace means receiving something from God that you don't deserve. No one deserves God's grace. In His eyes, everyone is a sinner. But God loves us, His children, and He provides grace to us through His gift of salvation. You can't do anything to earn grace. You receive it when you trust Jesus Christ as your Savior. Through faith in Him, God promises you the gift of eternal life in heaven. God's grace does not end there. He is constantly blessing you with gifts. His grace provides you with strength and guidance to face everyday life, and by grace He takes care of you, not only here on earth, but also someday in heaven. In what other ways has God shown you His grace?

Write God's Word on Your Heart Today

Short scripture verses are easy to memorize. Time yourself to see how long it takes you to remember this one:

For it is by grace you have been saved, through faith—
and this is not from yourselves, it is the gift of God.

EPHESIANS 2:8 NIV

Longer verses can be a bit more difficult, for example:

But he said to me, "My grace is sufficient for
you, for my power is made perfect in weakness."
Therefore I will boast all the more gladly about my
weaknesses, so that Christ's power may rest on me.

2 CORINTHIANS 12:9 NIV

With long memory verses, it sometimes helps to understand the verse in context. If you read 2 Corinthians 12:1–10, you will see that the writer is Paul. He writes about what he calls "a thorn" in his flesh. He does not reveal what it is but only says that it torments him. So Paul calls on the Lord for help. The Lord responds that His grace—His gift of being present with

Paul—is sufficient, and that His power is evident in the faith that Paul shows others in spite of his condition. God's answer makes Paul grateful for his thorn because by accepting it willingly he is a living example of faith and, therefore, serving God. Think about this scripture passage and its meaning. Then try memorizing 2 Corinthians 12:9. Break it down into manageable parts and memorize one part at a time until you commit it all to memory.

PATIENCE

Patience is better than too much pride. Only fools get angry quickly and hold a grudge.

ECCLESIASTES 7:8–9 CEV

After a hectic workday, Rachael wanted a relaxing evening at home. But it was Tuesday, her busiest night of the week. Rachael and her husband had Bible study at church, and their son and daughter both had music lessons. To make things easier for herself, Rachael decided to pick up dinner at a fast-food drive-through, something she rarely did. Several cars ahead of her had big orders, and Rachael's impatience swelled as the line inched along.

"What's the matter with these people?" she complained. "If I were in charge, things would run more smoothly." Later at Bible study, Rachael remembered her impatience and asked God for forgiveness.

Impatience leads to pride and anger, but patience results in kindness and self-control. Practicing patience every day will brighten not only your life but also the lives of others.

Write God's Word on Your Heart Today

Memorizing scripture requires time and patience, but it is well worth it. The more of God's Word you store in your heart, the better prepared you are for life's challenges and so much more. Second Timothy 3:16–17 (NIV) explains, "All Scripture is God-breathed and is useful for teaching, rebuking, correcting and training in righteousness, so that the servant of God may be thoroughly equipped for every good work."

Set aside a specific time for memorizing scripture when you won't be interrupted. Learn to be patient with yourself by not setting goals that will leave you feeling frustrated and dissatisfied. If you plan to memorize just one verse a day and then do two or three, good for you—you've exceeded your goal. But if anything gets in the way of your scripture memory time, react with patience. Remember, God is patient with you, much more patient than you deserve.

Memory verses:

The Lord isn't slow about keeping his promises, as some people think he is. In fact, God is patient, because he wants everyone to turn from sin and no one to be lost.

2 PETER 3:9 CEV

Be completely humble and gentle; be patient, bearing with one another in love.

EPHESIANS 4:2 NIV

But since I was worse than anyone else, God had mercy on me and let me be an example of the endless patience of Christ Jesus. He did this so that others would put their faith in Christ and have eternal life.

1 TIMOTHY 1:16 CEV

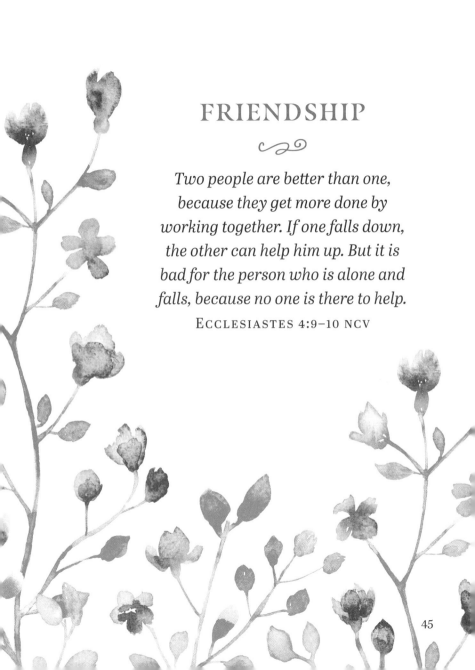

FRIENDSHIP

*Two people are better than one,
because they get more done by
working together. If one falls down,
the other can help him up. But it is
bad for the person who is alone and
falls, because no one is there to help.*

ECCLESIASTES 4:9–10 NCV

Your best friends hold a special place in your heart. They laugh with you, cry with you, and know you so well that they finish your sentences. Best friends are precious. There is one friend who will always be with you—now and through eternity—and His name is Jesus.

D. L. Moody, one of the greatest evangelists of the nineteenth century, said, "A rule I have had for years is: to treat the Lord Jesus Christ as a personal friend. His is not a creed, a mere doctrine, but it is He Himself we have." Do you have a personal relationship with Jesus? Let Him into your heart as you would your best friend, and allow Him to share every aspect of your life.

Write God's Word on Your Heart Today

The Bible holds many stories about friendship. You might want to study these verses about Ruth and Naomi (Ruth 1:16–17), David and Jonathan (1 Samuel 18:1–3), Job's friends (Job 2:11), and Elijah and Elisha (2 Kings 2:2). All are examples of friends loving and helping each other.

C. S. Lewis said, "Is any pleasure on earth as great as a circle of Christian friends by a good fire?" So invite a Christian friend— or two or three—to your home and help each other memorize some scripture. Try these ideas:

1. Read a verse to a friend and have her repeat it to you from memory.
2. Cite a specific chapter and verse. Then see if a friend can repeat it from memory. You can also set this up as a game of texting scripture citations to your friends and seeing if they know them. You might even assign points.
3. Discuss a verse before you and your friends try to memorize it. Thinking about the context helps you remember the words.

Begin with these memory verses:

So, you are not loyal to God! You should know that loving the world is the same as hating God. Anyone who wants to be a friend of the world becomes God's enemy.

JAMES 4:4 NCV

There are "friends" who destroy each other, but a real friend sticks closer than a brother.

PROVERBS 18:24 NLT

The heartfelt counsel of a friend is as sweet as perfume and incense.

PROVERBS 27:9 NLT

PRAYER

*Never stop praying, especially
for others. Always pray by the
power of the Spirit. Stay alert and
keep praying for God's people.*

Ephesians 6:18 CEV

It is awesome to know that God wants to communicate with us, not only as a group of believers but also as individuals. Prayer is the intimate connection that each of us has with God. We can speak directly to Him and know that He hears us.

God desires for us to have quiet time alone with Him in prayer. In Matthew 6:6 (NLT), Jesus gives these instructions: "When you pray, go away by yourself, shut the door behind you, and pray to your Father in private. Then your Father, who sees everything, will reward you." When you pray, your words need not be eloquent or rehearsed. Speak to God as you would to a loving father—because that is exactly who He is. God is your heavenly Father, and He is delighted whenever you come to Him in prayer.

Write God's Word on Your Heart Today

The twenty-third Psalm is a familiar scripture passage. You have probably learned it and can recite it from memory. Whenever you say it, you are praying to God. Praying the scriptures is a great way to memorize them. Having an arsenal of scripture prayers in your memory bank can help in those times when you have trouble finding the words to pray.

Look for scripture passages that work as prayers. The book of Psalms is a good place to begin. For example, learn and pray this scripture passage, Psalm 139:1–6 (NLT):

> *O LORD, you have examined my heart and know everything about me. You know when I sit down or stand up. You know my thoughts even when I'm far away. You see me when I travel and when I rest at home. You know everything I do. You know what I am going to say even before I say it, LORD. You go before me and follow me. You place your hand of blessing on my head. Such knowledge is too wonderful for me, too great for me to understand!*

Break the passage into small parts, learning one sentence at a time. After you have mastered it, incorporate it into your intimate prayer time with God.

Also, try learning Psalm 63:1–8. Read through the psalms, and you will find many that fit your daily needs.

PRIORITIES

*Love the L*ORD *your God with all
your heart and with all your soul
and with all your strength.*

DEUTERONOMY 6:5 NIV

David gained wisdom as his relationship with God grew deeper. He shared that wisdom in his writing. In Psalm 37:5 (NLT), he says, "Commit everything you do to the LORD. Trust him, and he will help you." David had learned an important lesson— make God your first priority.

Notice the words *commit everything*. Everything includes your time and relationships. Everything means God should come before your spouse, children, parents, extended family, church family, and the rest of the world. Put Him in control of every aspect of your life, and when you trust Him with everything, even the most insignificant things, God will help you. In verse 6 (NCV), David explains how God will change you when you make Him your first priority: "Your goodness will shine like the sun, and your fairness like the noonday sun." Trust Him today. Commit everything to God and make Him the head of your household.

Write God's Word on Your Heart Today

According to the *Oxford Dictionary of Proverbs*, the familiar idiom "The family that prays together stays together" was created by a writer of commercials, a man named Al Scalpone. It was broadcast in 1947 during the radio program *Family Theater of the Air*. The phrase caught on and has been used many times since.

Praying together, as well as studying the Bible and memorizing scripture together, can bring your family into a deeper relationship with God and each other. Set aside family time at least once a week to talk about and worship the Lord. Make scripture memory part of your worship time.

Short verses are easier for young children to remember. Begin with these verses about putting God first:

> *"Seek first God's kingdom and what God wants.*
> *Then all your other needs will be met as well."*
> MATTHEW 6:33 NCV

> *Do not worship any god except me.*
> EXODUS 20:3 CEV

*Love the Lord your God with all your
heart, soul, and mind. This is the first and
most important commandment.*
MATTHEW 22:37–38 CEV

Discuss what it means to put God first in everything. Ask family members to list other gods that they might be tempted to put before the one and only God—things like television, video games, friendships, and sports. Discuss why loving God with all your heart, soul, and mind is the most important commandment. Consider making a poster together that shows your family's priorities in order and cites the memory verses.

MARRIAGE

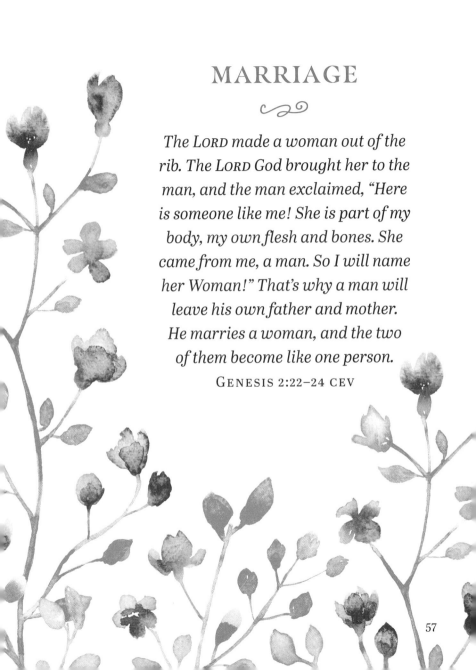

The LORD made a woman out of the rib. The LORD God brought her to the man, and the man exclaimed, "Here is someone like me! She is part of my body, my own flesh and bones. She came from me, a man. So I will name her Woman!" That's why a man will leave his own father and mother. He marries a woman, and the two of them become like one person.

GENESIS 2:22–24 CEV

The King James Version of the Bible mentions man and wife in the story of Adam and Eve in Genesis 2. The idea of marriage carries on through the Old Testament and is reinforced in the New Testament. Jesus repeated Genesis 2:22–24 when some Pharisees questioned Him about divorce. He added,"What God has joined together, let no one separate" (Mark 10:9 NIV).

Marriage is God's creation, designed for oneness, companionship, and intimacy. Think about marriage today. Are you and your spouse one and living according to God's commandments? Read Mark 10:1–12.

Write God's Word on Your Heart Today

Your relationship with your spouse ranks second to your relationship with God. Working together as partners joined as one heart focused on God is how marriage is supposed to work. By both of you putting God first and sharing Him fully with each other, you create oneness in your marriage. Sadly, today's marriages are not always God-centered. Insurance industry statistics estimate there are one million US divorces per year, listing the number one cause as lack of communication.

Time alone with your spouse is an important part of marriage, and nothing should get in the way of good, solid communication. A great way to center your marriage on God is to study the Bible and pray together daily. Start by helping each other memorize these scripture verses and discussing what they mean to you:

> *Each one of you also must love his wife as he loves himself, and the wife must respect her husband.*
> Ephesians 5:33 niv

59

In the same way, you husbands should live with your wives in an understanding way, since they are weaker than you. But show them respect, because God gives them the same blessing he gives you—the grace that gives true life. Do this so that nothing will stop your prayers.

1 PETER 3:7 NCV

Wives. . .submit yourselves to your own husbands so that, if any of them do not believe the word, they may be won over without words by the behavior of their wives.

1 PETER 3:1 NIV

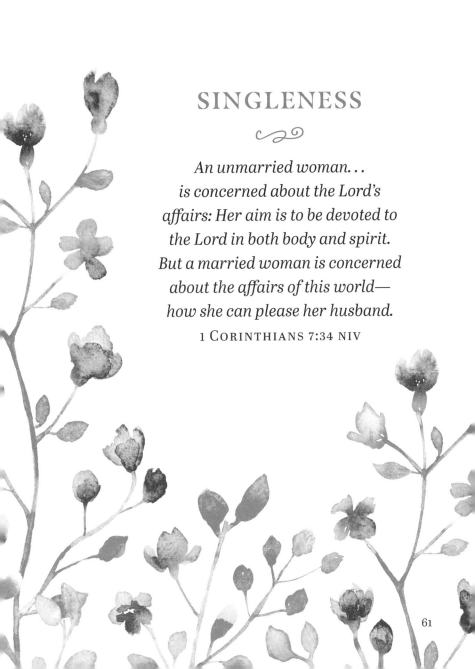

SINGLENESS

An unmarried woman...
is concerned about the Lord's
affairs: Her aim is to be devoted to
the Lord in both body and spirit.
But a married woman is concerned
about the affairs of this world—
how she can please her husband.

1 CORINTHIANS 7:34 NIV

It is no secret that the apostle Paul was an advocate for singleness. Paul believed that singleness allowed a person more time to devote to God.

Singleness is a matter of perception. It can be viewed as God's gift—Paul supposed that some are designed by God to remain single. Or, it can be viewed as a blight—some argue this using Genesis 2:18 (NIV), "The LORD God said, 'It is not good for the man to be alone. I will make a helper suitable for him.'"

The Bible treats marriage and singleness equally, a matter of choice. If you are single and eager to marry, ask God to provide peace in your singleness. Then wait patiently for Him to work out His plan for your life.

Write God's Word on Your Heart Today

Do you enjoy playing solitaire or working crossword puzzles? These kinds of activities make alone time more fun. You can make similar games to help memorize scripture.

Choose one of the following memory verses and write each word on a separate index card or small piece of paper. Then shuffle the pieces and put them together in the correct order. Do this until you know the verse by memory. Make it even more challenging by writing the words for all three verses and shuffling them together.

You can also create a game similar to Concentration. Spread out the word cards facedown in front of you. Turn over one card at a time. If it is the next word in the verse, keep it. If not, return it facedown. The object is to rebuild the memory verse in the correct word order.

Memory verses:

"For your Maker is your husband—the LORD Almighty is his name—the Holy One of Israel is your Redeemer; he is called the God of all the earth."

ISAIAH 54:5 NIV

"For my thoughts are not your thoughts, neither are your ways my ways," declares the LORD. "As the heavens are higher than the earth, so are my ways higher than your ways and my thoughts than your thoughts."

ISAIAH 55:8–9 NIV

So you also are complete through your union with Christ, who is the head over every ruler and authority.

COLOSSIANS 2:10 NLT

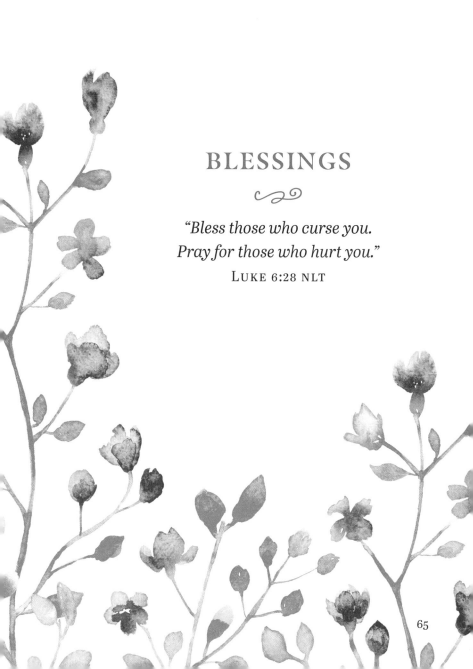

BLESSINGS

*"Bless those who curse you.
Pray for those who hurt you."*

LUKE 6:28 NLT

In Germany during the Nazi era, a Protestant Christian named Dietrich Bonhoeffer stood courageously to publicly oppose Adolf Hitler and his policies. Charged with conspiring to rescue Jews, Bonhoeffer was sent to a concentration camp and hanged. Witnesses to his death said that he died submissive to the will of God.

In his writings, Bonhoeffer defined blessing as "laying one's hand on something and saying: 'Despite everything, you belong to God.' This is what we do with the world that inflicts such suffering on us." Bonhoeffer believed that those blessed by God had the responsibility of passing that blessing along to others—even those who we think don't deserve it.

James 1:12 (NLT) says, "God blesses those who patiently endure testing and temptation. Afterward they will receive the crown of life that God has promised to those who love him." Will you receive such a crown? You might if, like Dietrich Bonhoeffer, you bless those who curse you.

Write God's Word on Your Heart Today

To be blessed means to be granted special favor by God. The following memory verses are important to remember because they help you think about and be grateful for God's blessings. The first verse is a blessing for you and the second is a blessing that you can share with others.

"But blessed is the one who trusts in the Lord, whose confidence is in him. They will be like a tree planted by the water that sends out its roots by the stream. It does not fear when heat comes; its leaves are always green. It has no worries in a year of drought and never fails to bear fruit."

JEREMIAH 17:7–8 NIV

"The Lord bless you and keep you; the Lord make his face shine on you and be gracious to you; the Lord turn his face toward you and give you peace."

NUMBERS 6:24–26 NIV

Scripture verses are sometimes incorporated into works of art. People use paintings, posters, quilts, embroidery, scrapbooking, and many other methods to blend scripture with creativity.

Think about the ways God has blessed you with creative talent. Then use your talents to share these verses with your family and friends. Will you sing them? Write them as poetry? Create a piece of art? However you choose, enjoy your time creating with the Creator and be blessed.

PEACE

You [God] will keep in perfect peace
those whose minds are steadfast,
because they trust in you.

ISAIAH 26:3 NIV

What is your idea of peace? Perhaps you find it when your children are asleep and you can rest. Or you might find peace while taking a long walk in the woods, soaking in a hot tub at the end of a hectic day, or unwinding with a cup of herbal tea and a good book. These are all peaceful ways to relax, but perfect peace is found only by giving all of your problems to God and leaving them there.

The prophet Isaiah provides simple instructions for perfect peace: set your mind to be steadfast on God, and trust Him. That word *steadfast* is key. It means "unmovable, firmly fixed in place." To attain perfect peace, you must be single-minded, fixing your thoughts only on God. Simple instructions, yet difficult to do.

Practice fixing your thoughts on God instead of your troubles. It takes work and repetition, but the reward is great.

Write God's Word on Your Heart Today

Throughout history, humans have searched for perfect peace. Most religions offer advice about how to find it. Many theories exist. But Christians believe that the only true route to perfect peace is complete trust in Jesus Christ—God. In the 1600s, the French Roman Catholic archbishop, theologian, and poet François Fénelon wrote: "Resign every forbidden joy; restrain every wish that is not referred to God's will; banish all eager desires, all anxiety; desire only the will of God; seek him alone and supremely, and you will find peace." In other words, make yours a God-centered life.

Memorizing scripture requires concentration and a peaceful environment. If you try to commit scripture to memory without your mind fixed on God, you might be memorizing the words without grasping their meaning or allowing them to sink into your heart. Find a peaceful place to memorize these three verses. Repeat them to yourself often throughout the day, always centering your thoughts on the Lord.

For God is not a God of confusion but of peace.

1 CORINTHIANS 14:33 ESV

In peace I will lie down and sleep, for you alone, LORD, make me dwell in safety.

PSALM 4:8 NIV

"Peace I leave with you; my peace I give you. I do not give to you as the world gives. Do not let your hearts be troubled and do not be afraid."

JOHN 14:27 NIV

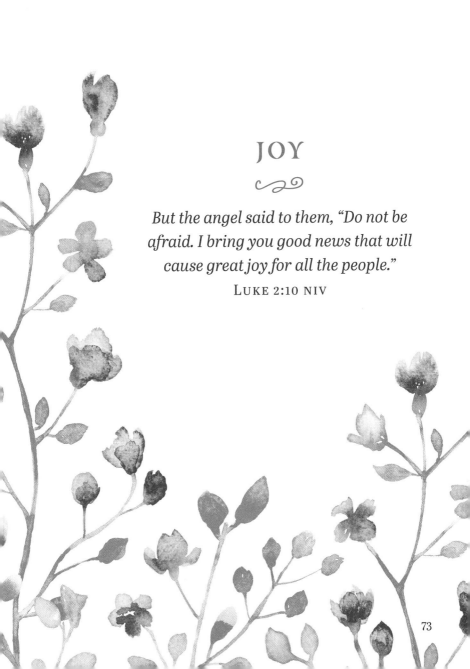

JOY

But the angel said to them, "Do not be afraid. I bring you good news that will cause great joy for all the people."

LUKE 2:10 NIV

The life and work of hymnist Isaac Watts echoes proof of 2 Corinthians 12:9 (NIV): "[The Lord said] 'My grace is sufficient for you, for my power is made perfect in weakness.' " Watts suffered from a psychiatric illness and an unsightly physical appearance. His biographers suggest that Watts proposed marriage to his sweetheart but was turned down. One source says, "Though she loved the jewel, she could not admire the casket which contained it." Despite illness and rejection, Watts' heart remained fixed on God. He wrote many well-known Christian hymns, including one of the happiest songs of Christmas, "Joy to the World."

When you feel unhappy, remember Watts's song. Remember that Jesus is the center of Christian joy. His birth signaled the beginning of God's salvation gift, and His death became the heart of joy—the joyful promise of eternal life—made perfect in imperfect circumstances.

Write God's Word on Your Heart Today

Oh, what joy there is in knowing the Lord!

Throughout the Bible people praise God with joyful songs. The word *joy* appears 165 times in the King James Version, and joyful singing has long been a staple of worship.

In Sunday school, children sing:

> *I've got the joy, joy, joy, joy down in my heart,*
> *Down in my heart, down in my heart,*
> *I've got the joy, joy, joy, joy down in my heart,*
> *Down in my heart to stay!*

In church, we sing hymns like "Joyful, Joyful, We Adore Thee."

In the psalms, David reminds worshippers to praise God with joyful songs. He says, in Psalm 33:3 (NLT), "Sing a new song of praise to [God]; play skillfully on the harp, and sing with joy."

Try singing some new songs of praise. Memorize the following verses by singing them. Make up your own melodies or sing the words using melodies from familiar songs.

This is the day that the Lord has made;
let us rejoice and be glad in it.

PSALM 118:24 ESV

I will be filled with joy because of you. I will
sing praises to your name, O Most High.

PSALM 9:2 NLT

I will sing about your power. Each morning I will sing
with joy about your unfailing love. For you have been
my refuge, a place of safety when I am in distress.

PSALM 59:16 NLT

COMFORT

When Job's. . .friends. . .heard about all the troubles that had come upon him, they set out from their homes and met together by agreement to go and sympathize with him and comfort him.

JOB 2:11 NIV

When they learned about Job's trouble, his friends hurried to be with him. The Bible says they went together to "sympathize with him and comfort him." That's what friends do—they provide comfort in troubled times. But sometimes, human comfort is not enough. This was true in Job's story. Although Job's friends tried to comfort him, their comfort was insufficient.

God knows that we need more than human comfort, so He sends us His Holy Spirit—the Comforter. The Holy Spirit provides help and comfort in our times of need and prays for us when we cannot find the words. Before He ascended to heaven, Jesus told His disciples, "I will not leave you comfortless: I will come to you" (John 14:18 KJV). His promise continues for all of us today. He comforts us through the Holy Spirit.

Write God's Word on Your Heart Today

The following memory scripture is quite long, so you might choose to incorporate some of the memory tips you have learned so far. Break the passage down sentence by sentence. Reflect on the meaning of each sentence. Focus on such key words as *praise, compassion, comfort,* and *abundantly.*

> *Praise be to the God and Father of our Lord Jesus Christ, the Father of compassion and the God of all comfort, who comforts us in all our troubles, so that we can comfort those in any trouble with the comfort we ourselves receive from God. For just as we share abundantly in the sufferings of Christ, so also our comfort abounds through Christ.*
>
> 2 CORINTHIANS 1:3–5 NIV

This scripture passage is an important one because it says so much about comfort. It tells us:

- God is the Father of compassion and the God of ALL Comfort.
- We should praise God for comforting us.

- We learn through God's comfort how to comfort others.
- We receive comfort abundantly through our Lord, Jesus Christ.

Remember this passage when you or a loved one needs comforting. Ask God to help and to lead you. If your own attempts to comfort fail and you are at a loss for words in prayer, you have assurance that the Holy Spirit will pray on your behalf. All you need to do is ask.

WOMANHOOD

*"Many women do noble things,
but you surpass them all."*

Proverbs 31:29 NIV

When an acquaintance asked Sue what she did for a living, Sue replied, "I'm Superwoman. I do everything." The world is filled with superwomen like Sue—women juggling work, family, household chores, and more. Perhaps you are one of them.

Proverbs 31:10–31 might well be renamed "Ode to a Superwoman." It provides insight into the lives of women in Old Testament times. Read it and you will see that not much has changed; the idea of a superwoman goes back thousand of years. Proverbs 31 tells of the many tasks women perform and points out that a woman of noble character who serves the Lord is worth far more than rubies. "Charm can be deceiving, and beauty fades away, but a woman who honors the LORD deserves to be praised. Show her respect—praise her in public for what she has done" (Proverbs 31:30–31 CEV).

So here's to superwomen everywhere! Praise God for women like you.

Write God's Word on Your Heart Today

Only 188 women are mentioned by name in the Bible. Some, like Ruth and Esther, have entire books devoted to their stories, but most are found tucked away in the scriptures. The Bible holds many stories, however brief, about women. Among them: Mary, the mother of Jesus; Mary Magdalene, Jesus' friend; the sisters Mary and Martha; Samuel's mother, Hannah; the prophetess, Anna; and Lydia, the Christian woman who sold purple cloth.

Plan a girls'-night-out Bible study with your friends to learn about some of the Bible's strongest women. You might read the book of Ruth and discuss Ruth's relationship with her mother-in-law, Naomi. Or read the book of Esther, and talk about how she saved her cousin Mordecai from death. Another idea is to assign each friend a woman in the Bible to research and share about at your Bible study.

Include these Proverbs 31 memory verses in your girls' night out:

A wife of noble character who can find? She is worth far more than rubies. Her husband has full confidence in her and lacks nothing of value. She brings him good, not harm, all the days of her life.

PROVERBS 31:10–12 NIV

She is strong and graceful, as well as cheerful about the future. Her words are sensible, and her advice is thoughtful. She takes good care of her family and is never lazy.

PROVERBS 31:25–27 CEV

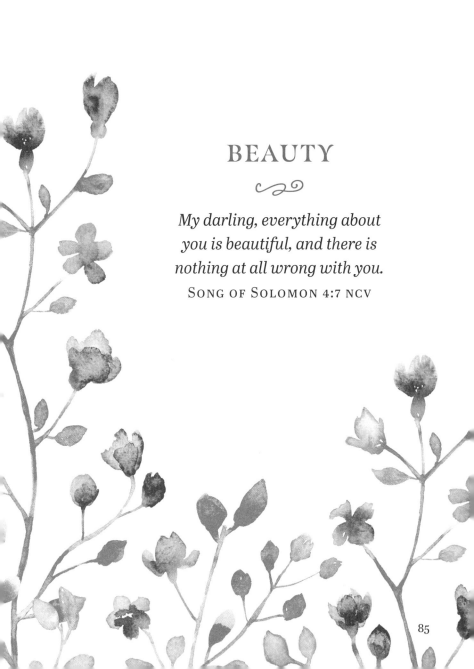

BEAUTY

*My darling, everything about
you is beautiful, and there is
nothing at all wrong with you.*

SONG OF SOLOMON 4:7 NCV

Do you always put on makeup before leaving the house? Statistics show that one in three women refuse to leave home without wearing makeup.

The idea of cosmetics and beauty treatments is nothing new. The book of Esther suggests that Esther prepared to meet her future husband, King Xerxes, with "twelve months of beauty treatments—six months with oil of myrrh, followed by six months with special perfumes and ointments. When it was time for her to go to the king's palace, she was given her choice of whatever clothing or jewelry she wanted to take from the harem" (Esther 2:12–13 NLT).

All through history, women have used cosmetics to enhance their good features and cover up flaws. But the truth is that there are no flaws. God made you perfectly beautiful in every way. Wherever you go, your outer beauty will never surpass the inner beauty of God's love shining through you.

Write God's Word on Your Heart Today

It is no secret that Eleanor Roosevelt was plain looking. The former first lady's looks were often made fun of in political cartoons and elsewhere, but instead of withdrawing in embarrassment, Eleanor Roosevelt became one of the most active and visible first ladies in history. She is quoted as saying, "No matter how plain a woman may be, if truth and honesty are written across her face, she will be beautiful."

Truth and honesty are part of the inner beauty that comes from knowing God. The Bible adds the traits of gentleness and quietness. It also reminds women, and men too, that God should be praised because He created them, and everything God does is perfect and right.

Make memorizing scripture part of your daily beauty routine. Write the following scripture passages on sticky notes, and stick them to the bathroom mirror or wherever you apply and remove your makeup:

*Don't depend on things like fancy hairdos or
gold jewelry or expensive clothes to make you
look beautiful. Be beautiful in your heart by
being gentle and quiet. This kind of beauty will
last, and God considers it very special.*

1 PETER 3:3–4 CEV

*[God,] You are the one who put me together inside
my mother's body, and I praise you because of
the wonderful way you created me. Everything
you do is marvelous! Of this I have no doubt.*

PSALM 139:13–14 CEV

Remember to tell yourself every day that you are
beautiful—and tell others that they are beautiful too!

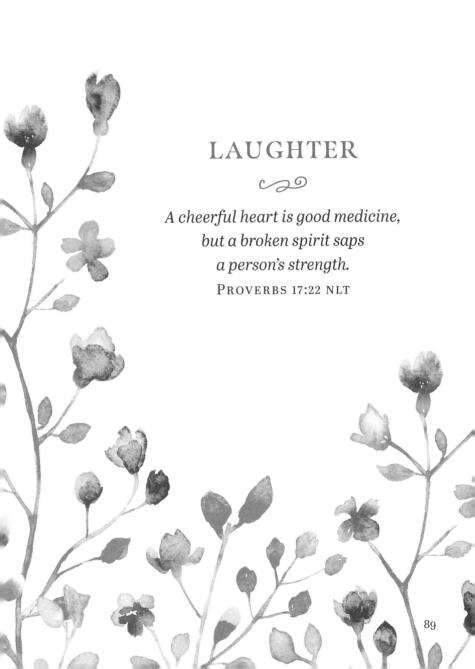

LAUGHTER

A cheerful heart is good medicine,
but a broken spirit saps
a person's strength.

PROVERBS 17:22 NLT

If Joyce's coworkers had to describe her in one word, it would be humorless. Joyce was no fun to work with. Nothing made her laugh. If anyone around her laughed, Joyce assumed that they were laughing at her. Do you know someone like Joyce? Some people live without seeing the humor in life and, least of all, in themselves.

Laughter, especially the ability to laugh at yourself, is a precious gift from God. Laughter and good, clean humor are healthy for the body and spirit. They create a cheerful heart, and the Bible calls a cheerful heart "good medicine." Laughter is meant to be shared. A good belly laugh can lift and help heal a broken spirit.

Look for the humor in life today. Laugh a little. Laugh a lot. Try to focus on the lighter side, and remember this: Blessed are those who can laugh at themselves, for they shall never cease to be amused!

Write God's Word on Your Heart Today

The Bible offers some great advice regarding humor and laughter:

1. It is good to make laughter a part of every day.

> *For the despondent, every day brings trouble;*
> *for the happy heart, life is a continual feast.*
> PROVERBS 15:15 NLT

2. God wants you to laugh and enjoy life, but be careful what you choose as the source of your happiness.

Be cheerful and enjoy life while you are young! Do what
you want and find pleasure in what you see. But don't
forget that God will judge you for everything you do.
ECCLESIASTES 11:9 CEV

3. There is a right way to tell jokes.

> *Don't use dirty or foolish or filthy words.*
> EPHESIANS 5:4 CEV

4. There is a right time and place to laugh.

A sensible person mourns, but fools always laugh.
ECCLESIASTES 7:4 CEV

5. When you feel sad, you can trust God to dry your tears.

God will bless you people who are
now crying. You will laugh!
LUKE 6:21 CEV

Plan a family night with humor as its theme. Share jokes and funny stories with each other or play a silly game. Choose one of the scripture verses on this page to memorize together. Discuss the verse and ask each family member to tell how it relates to his or her life. End your family night with a prayer, and thank God for blessing your family with laughter.

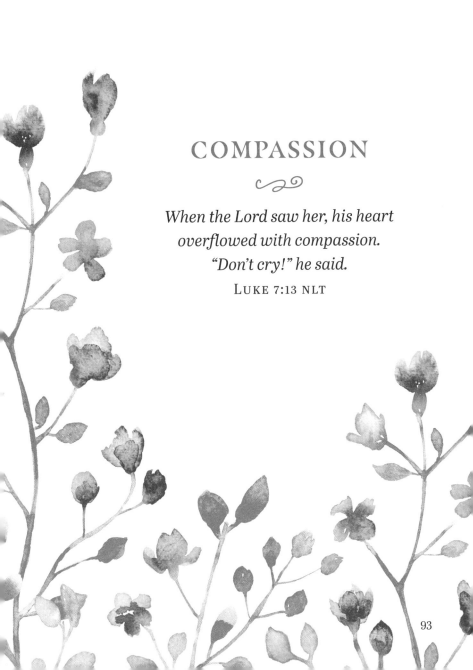

COMPASSION

*When the Lord saw her, his heart
overflowed with compassion.
"Don't cry!" he said.*

LUKE 7:13 NLT

93

A dozen runners stood ready at the starting line. All the young women with special needs had trained hard for the race. Each dreamed of winning the gold in the Special Olympics. With a pistol's crack, they sprinted toward the finish line.

Then it happened. One of them fell. She hit the asphalt hard, lay there, and cried. Two runners saw her fall and at that moment they had to choose. Should they stop and help their competitor or keep running? They stopped. The girls gave up their dreams of winning to comfort someone in need.

Imagine willingly giving up something you've really wanted. Jesus put aside His own desires to help those who followed Him and to heal their sicknesses. Then He made the ultimate sacrifice and gave up His life. Jesus' heart overflowed with compassion, and yours should too. Do you know someone who has fallen down? How can you help today?

Write God's Word on Your Heart Today

Compassion is a feeling of wanting to help someone, but compassion has another element—awareness. Compassion is the result of looking around you and becoming aware of needs.

Do you know someone who needs help memorizing scripture? Some people find it difficult to commit a specific set of words to memory. Maybe you can help by sharing some of the memorization tips you have learned.

It might be helpful to create questions about the key idea of a specific verse and then quiz yourself or a friend. Once the main idea is familiar, it becomes easier to remember a verse. Try it with these:

Can you name the four characteristics of God found in Psalm 86:15?

But you, O Lord, are a God of compassion
and mercy, slow to get angry and filled
with unfailing love and faithfulness.

PSALM 86:15 NLT

What does 1 John 3:17 say about God's love and compassion?

*If someone has enough money to live well and
sees a brother or sister in need but shows no
compassion— how can God's love be in that person?*

1 JOHN 3:17 NLT

Why did Jesus have compassion on the crowd in Mark 6:34?
What did He do to help them?

*Jesus saw the huge crowd as he stepped from the
boat, and he had compassion on them because
they were like sheep without a shepherd. So
he began teaching them many things.*

MARK 6:34 NLT

What other questions might you ask about these verses?

ENCOURAGEMENT

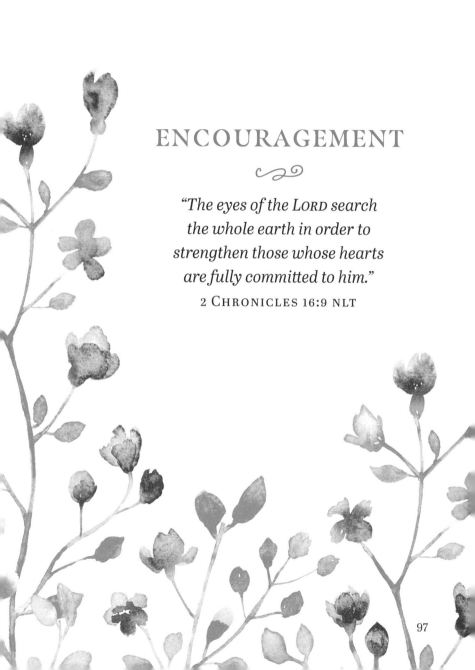

*"The eyes of the LORD search
the whole earth in order to
strengthen those whose hearts
are fully committed to him."*

2 CHRONICLES 16:9 NLT

"I believe in you!"

"You can do it!"

"I love the way you did that!"

God shouts similar phrases to you every day, but your heart must be quiet to hear Him. In 2 Chronicles 16:9, the Bible says that God roams the earth searching for people to encourage. Zephaniah 3:17 (NCV) suggests that when God encourages someone, He stays with them and gives them confidence: "The LORD your God is with you; the mighty One will save you." God also acts as a cheerleader: "He will rejoice over you." And when you accomplish something great, He will shower you with compliments: "You will rest in his love; he will sing and be joyful about you."

Encouragement is powerful. If it wasn't, would God roam the planet shouting accolades to His children? Learn from His actions. Be an encourager often, each and every day.

Write God's Word on Your Heart Today

The author and theologian J. I. Packer is quoted as saying, "The stars may fall, but God's promises will stand and be fulfilled." The Bible is full of God's encouraging promises—there are more than three thousand of them! Of course, it would be almost impossible to memorize them all, but there is nothing wrong with a little friendly competition, and that includes competing to memorize scripture.

Try this. Challenge a friend to a scripture memory contest. You might begin with a written list of scriptures and a set amount of time; then see which of you can be the first to commit all the verses to memory. Or, you might see which of you can create the longest list of encouraging scripture verses and then help each other memorize some of them. Whichever method you choose, remember to encourage and compliment one another. Here are several verses to get you started:

"Believe in the Lord Jesus and you will be saved,
along with everyone in your household."

ACTS 16:31 NLT

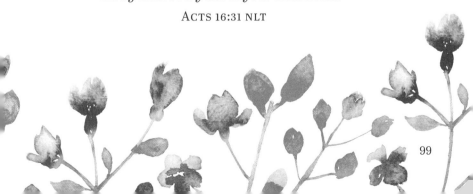

This is the confidence we have in approaching God:
that if we ask anything according
to his will, he hears us.

1 JOHN 5:14 NIV

"Be strong and courageous. Do not be afraid or
terrified. . .for the LORD your God goes with you;
he will never leave you nor forsake you."

DEUTERONOMY 31:6 NIV

SLEEP

*Look up into the heavens. Who
created all the stars? He brings
them out like an army, one after
another, calling each by its name.*

Isaiah 40:26 NLT

Do you have trouble sleeping? Many women complain that when they go to bed their minds reel with thoughts and worries.

Sleep does not come easy when your mind is fixed on the world. If you cannot sleep, try setting your thoughts on the heavens. The clear night sky confirms the wonders of God. The prophet Isaiah said that not only did God create the stars, but also He knows exactly how many there are, and He even has names for them all. You can find comfort knowing that when you sleep God rules the universe, and He watches over you as well. Jesus said, "Come to me, all of you who are tired and have heavy loads, and I will give you rest" (Matthew 11:28 NCV). So give your thoughts and worries to Him, and enjoy a good night's sleep.

Write God's Word on Your Heart Today

"Rest in the Lord," says David, the psalmist (Psalm 37:7 KJV). Don't fret! And he adds this advice in Psalm 37:7–8 (NCV): "Don't be upset when others get rich or when someone else's plans succeed. Don't get angry. Don't be upset; it only leads to trouble."

God knows that His people fret. They fret about work situations and about their families. Financial issues, health problems, detailed plans, anticipation, to-do lists—all of these lead to fretting, trouble, and sleeplessness.

The truth is that no one needs to worry and fret, because God has everything under control. God never sleeps. He is everywhere, all the time, watching over His children.

You can combat sleeplessness by memorizing the following verses from Psalms. Recite them to yourself when fretting keeps you awake at night. By doing so, you will teach yourself to focus on God instead of your troubles.

It is useless for [me] to work so hard from early morning until late at night, anxiously working for food to eat; for God gives rest to his loved ones.

PSALM 127:2 NLT

[God,] on my bed I remember you; I think of you through the watches of the night.

PSALM 63:6 NIV

Truly my soul finds rest in God; my salvation comes from him.

PSALM 62:1 NIV

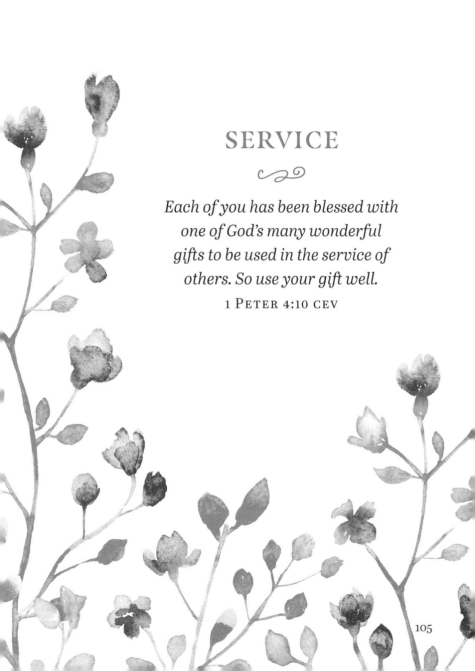

SERVICE

Each of you has been blessed with one of God's many wonderful gifts to be used in the service of others. So use your gift well.

1 Peter 4:10 cev

God blesses everyone with gifts useful for service. Some gifts are obvious. Others are waiting to be discovered. Maybe you sing in the church choir. Have you thought that your voice serves others? Not only does it entertain, but also it brings hearts nearer to God.

Gifts of service come in many forms. In the Bible, Ruth's gift was providing companionship and care for her mother-in-law, Naomi. God blessed Abigail, Nabal's wife, with intelligence. She used her wisdom well and knew how to execute her plans. Anna had the gift of prayer and prophecy. Even in her old age, she spent day and night in the temple worshipping and praying.

Take time today to think about your gifts, and decide how you can use them to serve others.

Write God's Word on Your Heart Today

Maybe you prefer a simple, straightforward plan for memorizing scripture—a plan with a specific set of steps that can be repeated the same way each day.

Try this:

1. Find a quiet place with no distractions.
2. Ask God to help you understand and memorize the verse.
3. Memorize the scripture reference first.
4. Next, read the verse aloud, slowly, several times.
5. Now, focus on memorizing key words.
6. On a notecard, write the scripture reference on one side and the verse on the other. Put the card reference-side up in a place where you will see it often throughout the day.
7. Whenever you look at the card, try to repeat the verse. Do this until you have committed the verse to memory.

Using this method, try memorizing these verses about serving others:

If you have the gift of speaking, preach God's message. If you have the gift of helping others, do it with the strength that God supplies. Everything should be done in a way that will bring honor to God because of Jesus Christ, who is glorious and powerful forever. Amen.

1 PETER 4:11 CEV

My friends, you were chosen to be free. So don't use your freedom as an excuse to do anything you want. Use it as an opportunity to serve each other with love.

GALATIANS 5:13 CEV

FORGIVENESS

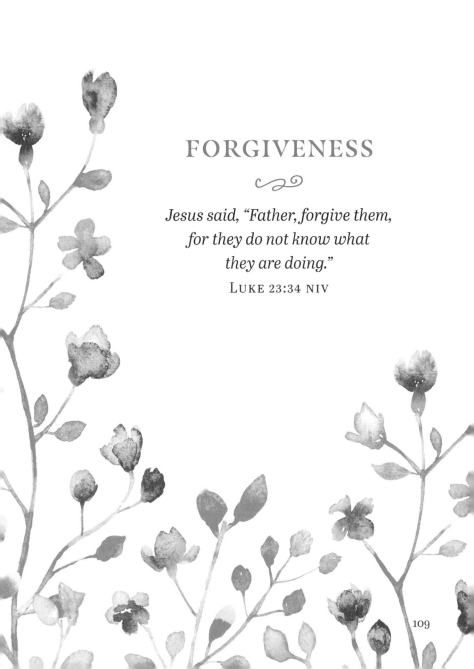

*Jesus said, "Father, forgive them,
for they do not know what
they are doing."*

LUKE 23:34 NIV

God requires forgiveness from His people. Sometimes forgiveness is easy, but just as often it is not. Hurtful words, cruel actions, and a lack of empathy all make forgiveness tough.

Television newscasts feature stories of unlikely forgiveness: a mother forgives her son's killer, a person seriously injured in a crash forgives the drunk driver who caused the accident, an adopted child forgives the parents who gave her away. All of these stories inspire us and lead us to ask, "Could I be as forgiving?"

When forgiveness is hard, you can remember Jesus suffering and dying on the cross for you. In His agony, He thought of you. He asked God to forgive His killers—to forgive you! This is God's example of forgiveness. Think about it. Could you be as forgiving as Jesus? Can you forgive those who hurt you?

Write God's Word on Your Heart Today

There are many creative ways to blend crafts and hobbies with memorizing scripture. You might write a memory verse in a journal and then write about how it applies to your life. Or if you do calligraphy or enjoy using different computer fonts, you could write the verse using a unique design. You can make a scrapbook journal of memory verses, or if you enjoy needlecrafts, you can incorporate the verse or parts of it into embroidery or an article of clothing. Woodworking, banners, stencils. . .there are endless possibilities.

Choose one of the following verses to memorize. Then use your creativity to share it with others.

"The Lord our God is merciful and forgiving,
even though we have rebelled against him."

Daniel 9:9 NIV

Get rid of all bitterness, rage, anger, harsh words, and slander, as well as all types of evil behavior. Instead, be kind to each other, tenderhearted, forgiving one another, just as God through Christ has forgiven you.

EPHESIANS 4:31–32 NLT

Then Peter came to him and asked, "Lord, how often should I forgive someone who sins against me? Seven times?" "No, not seven times," Jesus replied, "but seventy times seven!"

MATTHEW 18:21–22 NLT

"If you forgive those who sin against you, your heavenly Father will forgive you."

MATTHEW 6:14 NLT

TEMPTATION

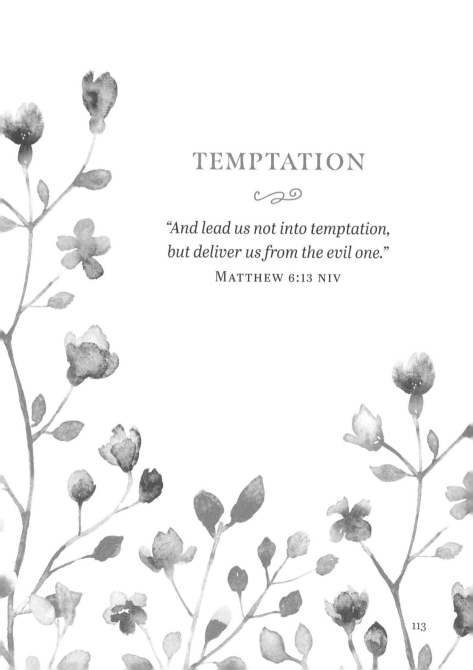

*"And lead us not into temptation,
but deliver us from the evil one."*

MATTHEW 6:13 NIV

Everyone faces temptation. It might be that extra cookie that tempts you to betray your diet or that sweater on sale at your favorite store that tempts you to betray your budget.

Satan loves it when God's people surrender to temptation. We read in the Bible that Samson gave in to Delilah's seduction. Ultimately that led to Samson's downfall and death. David had a similar encounter with temptation, but he repented and was saved. And, of course, there is the story of Eve's temptation in the Garden of Eden that led to all our worldly sins. Giving in when you know you should not is helping the enemy and betraying God.

Satan promised Jesus the world if He turned from God and worshipped him. But Jesus answered, "Worship the Lord your God and serve him only" (Luke 4:8 NIV). That is the response you should have when temptation stands in your way.

Write God's Word on Your Heart Today

Is Satan tempting you to skip memorizing these verses? If so, you are not alone. Satan tempts everyone to avoid serving God. And memorizing scripture, writing it on our hearts, is one way that we serve Him.

There are things that you can do when you face temptation:

1. Pray. Ask God to help you stay focused on Him and what He wants you to do.
2. Stop and reflect. Ask yourself, "What am I about to do?" Decide whether giving in to temptation aligns with what you know is God's will.
3. Do it right away. When tempted not to do something that you know you should do—like memorizing scripture—do it right away! Procrastination is giving in to temptation.
4. Get an accountability partner. Ask a friend or family member to join you in memorizing scripture. Hold each other accountable to complete the task.
5. Memorize the following verses! Allow them to sink into your heart, and repeat them when Satan tries to divert you from God.

"Watch and pray so that you will not fall into temptation. The spirit is willing, but the flesh is weak."

MATTHEW 26:41 NIV

No temptation has overtaken you except what is common to mankind. And God is faithful; he will not let you be tempted beyond what you can bear. But when you are tempted, he will also provide a way out so that you can endure it.

1 CORINTHIANS 10:13 NIV

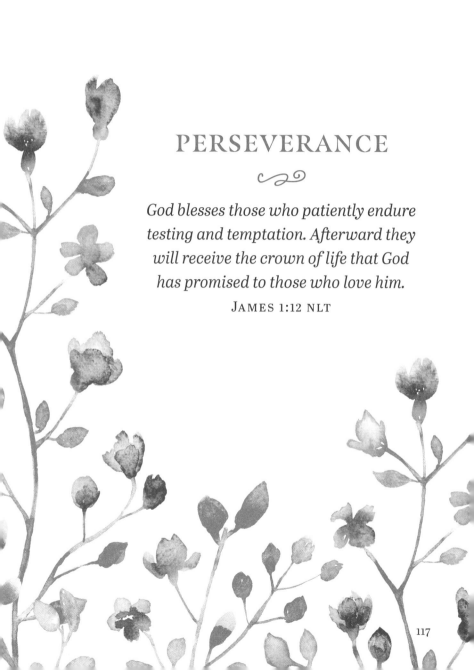

PERSEVERANCE

God blesses those who patiently endure testing and temptation. Afterward they will receive the crown of life that God has promised to those who love him.

JAMES 1:12 NLT

Diann received a frightening diagnosis. She had ovarian cancer. The odds of surviving were unfavorable. Surgery, chemotherapy, and radiation still left Diann with a very poor prognosis, but she persevered. She listened to her doctors and endured her treatments without complaining. More importantly, she put all of her trust in God. She moved forward, steadfast and strong. Now, five years later, Diann continues to face cancer with faith. She perseveres, spending her days encouraging others and winning souls for Christ. Despite her illness, Diann refuses to give up until she receives the crown of life that God promises her in heaven.

Perseverance means remaining steadfast under pressure and patiently enduring trouble. Are you facing troubles today? With patience, put all of your faith and trust in God, and He will reward you with blessings.

Write God's Word on Your Heart Today

There are many Dianns in the world, Christians enduring trials through perseverance. They inspire and aid us in having our own courage to persevere.

Oswald Chambers, theologian and author of *My Utmost for His Highest*, wrote, "Perseverance is more than endurance. It is endurance combined with absolute assurance and certainty that what we are looking for is going to happen." Naturally, we want whatever we are looking for to happen soon and while we are still here on earth. But if God decides otherwise, then we have assurance that a great outcome is awaiting us in heaven. Perseverance is fixing our thoughts on moving forward toward that goal.

The apostle Paul was a champion of perseverance. He endured shipwrecks, imprisonment, beatings, cold winters, and persecution because of his Christianity. He never gave up. Paul died still facing trials. Some scholars suggest that he was beheaded because he refused to deny his faith.

Today's memory verse comes from Paul. Persevere until you have learned it. Store it in your heart to remember when trouble comes your way.

Let your faith be like a shield, and you will be able to stop all the flaming arrows of the evil one. Let God's saving power be like a helmet, and for a sword use God's message that comes from the Spirit. Never stop praying, especially for others. Always pray by the power of the Spirit. Stay alert and keep praying for God's people.

EPHESIANS 6:16–18 CEV

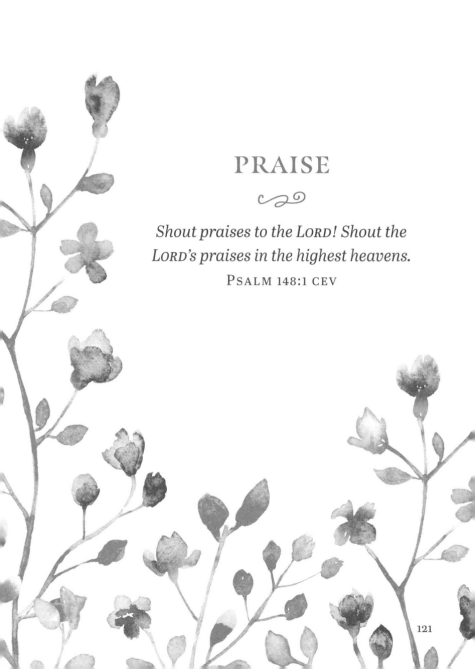

PRAISE

*Shout praises to the Lord! Shout the
Lord's praises in the highest heavens.*

Psalm 148:1 cev

Who should praise God? In Psalm 148, the psalmist answers by way of a list: angels and those who serve God in heaven, the sun, moon, stars, and the water in the heavens, all creatures on earth as well as sea monsters, fire and hail, snow, frost, and the wind, mountains and hills, fruit and cedar trees, every tame and wild animal, reptiles and birds, every king, ruler, and nation, and every man and woman, young or old. He could have gone on forever making his list, but the psalmist ends it with this all-encompassing phrase: "All creation, come praise the name of the LORD" (Psalm 148:13 CEV).

Everyone and everything are to praise God. Why? Because God is the great Creator. He made everyone and every good thing. We praise God because He protects us and we belong to Him. His glory—His wonderfulness—is greater than anything on earth or in heaven. So praise Him. Shout praises to the Lord!

Write God's Word on Your Heart Today

One reason for memorizing scripture is to use it to praise God in prayer. A perfect example of a praise prayer is this one from King David in 1 Chronicles 29:10–13 (NIV):

> *"Praise be to you, LORD, the God of our father Israel, from everlasting to everlasting. Yours, LORD, is the greatness and the power and the glory and the majesty and the splendor, for everything in heaven and earth is yours. Yours, LORD, is the kingdom; you are exalted as head over all. Wealth and honor come from you; you are the ruler of all things. In your hands are strength and power to exalt and give strength to all. Now, our God, we give you thanks, and praise your glorious name. [Amen.]"*

Praising God through prayer is an effective way of drawing nearer to Him. Memorize these scriptures to use in your own praise prayer:

You changed my sorrow into dancing. You took away my clothes of sadness, and clothed me in happiness. I will sing to you and not be silent. Lord, my God, I will praise you forever.

PSALM 30:11–12 NCV

Because your love is better than life, my lips will glorify you. I will praise you as long as I live, and in your name I will lift up my hands.

PSALM 63:3–4 NIV

MOTHERHOOD

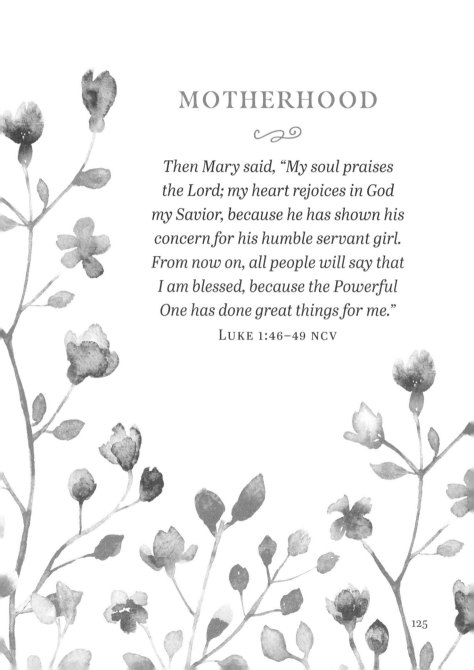

*Then Mary said, "My soul praises
the Lord; my heart rejoices in God
my Savior, because he has shown his
concern for his humble servant girl.
From now on, all people will say that
I am blessed, because the Powerful
One has done great things for me."*

LUKE 1:46–49 NCV

Imagine discovering that God chose you to be His Son's mother. This was Mary's blessing, and a wonderful blessing it was. Still, she remained humble. Mary did what God requires of all mothers. She loved Jesus and did her best for Him.

If God has chosen you for motherhood, He has entrusted you with an important responsibility. Whether your child is a famous movie star or an overlooked, unemployed student, your role as a mother is the same, to be the best mother you can be and to raise your child to love Jesus. Motherhood is God's gift to you. It means that He trusts you with His most precious creation, a child—*His* child—and like Mary, you are blessed.

Write God's Word on Your Heart Today

Helping your child memorize Bible verses is rewarding and fun. Even preschoolers are able to memorize simple scripture verses like:

"Do to others as you would like them to do to you."
LUKE 6:31 NLT

This day belongs to the LORD! Let's celebrate and be glad today.
PSALM 118:24 CEV

Children must always obey their parents. This pleases the Lord.
COLOSSIANS 3:20 CEV

Plan for your child to memorize one verse per week. Make memorization fun. You can turn a memory verse into a song or play a game in which you and your child repeat the verse back and forth to each other. Incorporate the verse into your daily conversations and discuss it at the dinner table. Ask your child to recite the verse before her bedtime prayers.

Now, here are two verses for you to memorize. They will help you to remember that children are a blessing and that you have been entrusted by God to train them well in a Christian home.

Children are a gift from the LORD;
they are a reward from him.

PSALM 127:3 NLT

"And you must love the LORD your God with all your
heart, all your soul, and all your strength. And you must
commit yourselves wholeheartedly to these commands
that I am giving you today. Repeat them again and
again to your children. Talk about them when you
are at home and when you are on the road, when
you are going to bed and when you are getting up."

DEUTERONOMY 6:5–7 NLT

LOVING OTHERS

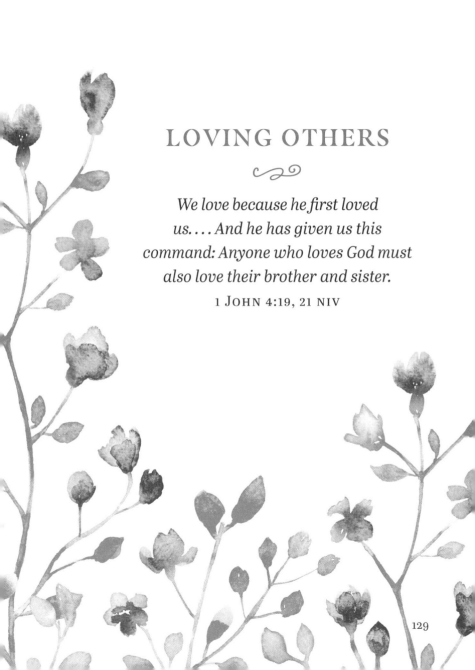

We love because he first loved us.... And he has given us this command: Anyone who loves God must also love their brother and sister.

1 John 4:19, 21 NIV

Joel, a bright eighteen-year-old boy, looked forward to completing his last semester in high school and attending college in the fall. But those plans changed dramatically on a snowy New Year's Day when a snowboarding accident nearly killed Joel and left him with brain damage. This once vibrant young man became withdrawn, belligerent, unkind, and selfish. His parents and brothers did their best to love him, but some days loving Joel was a challenge.

God understands that sometimes people are difficult to love. This is why He reminds us to love others because He loves us. All of us are difficult, sinful children of God. Still, God loves us. There is nothing we can do that will separate us from His love. So, when loving someone becomes a challenge, open your heart and allow God's love to flow through you.

Write God's Word on Your Heart Today

If you don't use something for a while, it gathers dust. The same applies for scripture verses written on your heart. If you don't use them, they become lost under layers of debris. It is one thing to memorize a passage of scripture and another to put it into action.

When memorizing scripture, always consider how it applies to you personally. Ask God to show you how He wants you to use the scripture to enrich your life or the lives of others. Then, put scripture into action.

Sometimes acting on scripture is an inward task, doing something to improve your Christian character. At other times, acting on scripture is an outward activity as you help or care for others.

A helpful method of acting on scripture is to choose one Bible verse each week as a memory-action verse. Spend the first day memorizing and meditating on the scripture and the rest of the week putting it into action.

Here are two verses to get you started:

Do nothing out of selfish ambition or vain conceit. Rather, in humility value others above yourselves, not looking to your own interests but each of you to the interests of the others.

PHILIPPIANS 2:3–4 NIV

Each of us should please our neighbors for their good, to build them up.

ROMANS 15:2 NIV

LOVING GOD

"Love the Lord your God with all your heart and with all your soul and with all your strength and with all your mind."

Luke 10:27 niv

Jesus visited His friends Mary and Martha. While Martha worked hard preparing a meal, her sister sat with Jesus listening to what He said. You can imagine how Martha felt working in the kitchen while her sister did nothing to help. Maybe you have experienced something similar in your own home.

Finally, Martha had had enough. She asked Jesus to agree with her: "Lord, don't you care that my sister has left me to do the work by myself? Tell her to help me!"

Jesus' answer might have surprised her. "Martha. . .you are worried and upset about many things, but few things are needed—or indeed only one. Mary has chosen what is better, and it will not be taken away from her" (Luke 10:40–42 NIV).

Loving God requires *all* of your heart, soul, strength, and mind. Do you love Him enough to always put Him first?

Write God's Word on Your Heart Today

One can only imagine whether Martha might have procrastinated about memorizing scripture. Like many women today, she had a to-do list, and when her friend Jesus came to visit, at the top of Martha's list was making a delicious meal for Him. Perhaps it was because Jesus was a close friend, someone whom Martha felt comfortable with, that she was so frank with Him. "Tell her to help me!" Could you be that casual with Jesus?

We forget, sometimes, that Jesus is not only our Lord but also our friend. We should always treat Him with respect, but we can talk with Jesus as openly as we talk to a beloved friend. He should be our best friend, our dearest and most loved friend.

Set aside your to-do list today, and make memorizing scripture your priority. Reading God's words and keeping them in your heart is a wonderful way to show Jesus that you love Him.

But as it is written in the Scriptures: "No one has ever seen this, and no one has ever heard about it. No one has ever imagined what God has prepared for those who love him."

1 CORINTHIANS 2:9 NCV

*"Those who know my commands and obey them
are the ones who love me, and my Father will
love those who love me. I will love them
and will show myself to them."*

JOHN 14:21 NCV

WISDOM

Do not reject me when I am old; do not leave me when my strength is gone.

PSALM 71:9 NCV

The Alzheimer's had advanced to where Pam was like a stranger to her mother. Pam dreaded the nursing home visits where she sat with her mom, neither of them speaking. Then, one day, an angel paid them a visit. Her name was Eleanor.

Eleanor was a resident at the home, eighty-eight years young with a mind sharp as a thirty-year-old woman. "Honey, your mother is still here," she said. "Talk to her and hold her hand."

Whenever Pam visited her mother, Eleanor sat with them. They became friends. Always, Eleanor held Pam's mother's hand and stroked it gently. As Pam watched her mom respond to Eleanor's touch and her soft, kind words, she learned to reconnect with her mother in a brand-new way. "It's like Jesus is sitting here with us," she said.

God blesses the elderly with many years of wisdom. Listen to them and learn. You might discover an angel in disguise.

Write God's Word on Your Heart Today

Wisdom comes from God's Word and also from His teachers. God's teachers are not just in classrooms and churches. They exist everywhere. You might be surprised that not all of them are believers. God can use anyone as a teacher. You gain wisdom from rejection, misunderstanding, and pain just as much as you do from acceptance, understanding, and joy. God's lessons can be soft or hard, but all of them make you wiser.

The elderly can be excellent teachers. Consider volunteering to lead a scripture memory and discussion group at your church or at a senior center. Listen and learn from what older adults have to share. They might have insight into scripture that is very different from your own. And they will learn from you to see the world from another point of view.

Find an older partner, and memorize these verses together:

"Older people are wise, and long life brings understanding."
JOB 12:12 NCV

Even though I am old and gray, do not leave me, God. I will tell the children about your power; I will tell those who live after me about your might.

PSALM 71:18 NCV

"Getting wisdom is the wisest thing you can do! And whatever else you do, develop good judgment."

PROVERBS 4:7 NLT

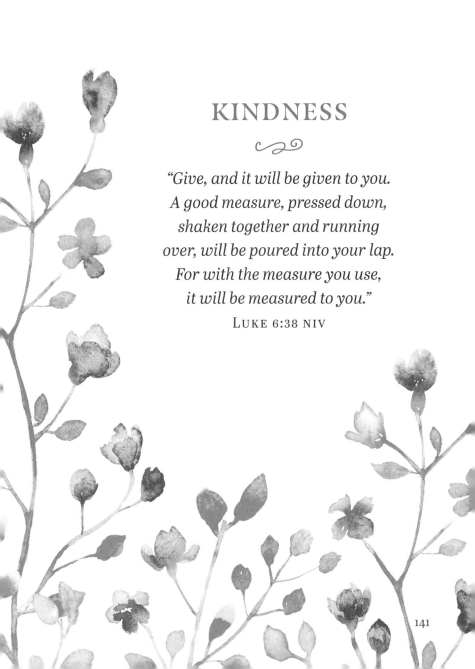

KINDNESS

"Give, and it will be given to you.
A good measure, pressed down,
shaken together and running
over, will be poured into your lap.
For with the measure you use,
it will be measured to you."

LUKE 6:38 NIV

Kind acts are often unexpected. A love note tucked into a lunch-box or a container of chicken soup brought to a sick friend is sure to result in a smile. God sees and smiles when you feed a stranger's parking meter or return a misplaced shopping cart to the store. A little kindness goes a long way.

Billy Graham said, "Often the only thing a child can remember about an adult in later years, when he or she is grown, is whether or not that person was kind." Are you the sort of adult that children will remember for kindness? Practice kindness. Make it a habit. Then watch as kindness returns to you—a good measure, pressed down, shaken together, and running over!

Write God's Word on Your Heart Today

Creating your own tips and tricks for memorizing scripture can be fun.

Marsha discovered that she walked the same routes through her house every day, so she created a scripture memory route game. Using index cards, she wrote one word of a memory verse on each card. Then she taped the cards in word order along a path (kitchen to upstairs bedroom, living room to laundry room, etc.). As Marsha walked the route, she read and memorized the verse.

Rochelle linked scripture memorization with her passion for chocolate. She allowed herself one scrumptious chocolate treat every day, but only after she memorized *three* Bible verses. Sometimes she changed the game to memorize the verses before she could watch her favorite television show or read the next chapter in a good book.

Lisa memorized entire psalms while walking on a treadmill. And Lauren sometimes opened her Bible to a random page, closed her eyes, allowed her index finger to rest anywhere on the page, and then memorized the verse it pointed to.

See if you can create a unique way to memorize these verses:

If your gift is to encourage others, be encouraging. If it is giving, give generously. If God has given you leadership ability, take the responsibility seriously. And if you have a gift for showing kindness to others, do it gladly.

ROMANS 12:8 NLT

When she speaks, her words are wise, and she gives instructions with kindness.

PROVERBS 31:26 NLT

UNDERSTANDING

Trust in the LORD with all your heart; do not depend on your own understanding. Seek his will in all you do, and he will show you which path to take.

PROVERBS 3:5–6 NLT

God, I don't understand.

I don't understand why I didn't get that job. I don't understand why my finances are such a mess. I don't understand why I can't get pregnant.

Many things are beyond our human understanding, and then we cry out to God: *Why?*

The answer might not come readily or be clear. Paul says, "Now we see things imperfectly, like puzzling reflections in a mirror, but then we will see everything with perfect clarity. All that I know now is partial and incomplete, but then I will know everything completely, just as God now knows me completely" (1 Corinthians 13:12 NLT).

When you accept that you can't understand God's ways and put all of your trust in His perfect will, He promises to lead you down His path to *why*. Trust Him. He has all the answers.

Write God's Word on Your Heart Today

An unexpected or unpleasant event can turn your life upside down. That's when it is most important to search your heart for the scripture verses you have memorized and stored there.

Scripture is helpful because it is God speaking directly to you. Jesus said:

> *"To those who listen to my teaching, more understanding will be given, and they will have an abundance of knowledge. But for those who are not listening, even what little understanding they have will be taken away from them."*
>
> MATTHEW 13:12 NLT

Scripture is helpful because it helps you to pray.

> *Give me understanding and I will obey your instructions; I will put them into practice with all my heart.*
>
> PSALM 119:34 NLT

Scripture is helpful because it provides advice.

Tune your ears to wisdom, and
concentrate on understanding.
PROVERBS 2:2 NLT

Commit these verses to memory. Carry them with you in your heart. Write them down. Put them where you will see them. Then when life hits hard you will remember—God understands everything. He knows exactly what happened and why. He loves you and He understands you. He knows better than you, or anyone else, what should happen next.

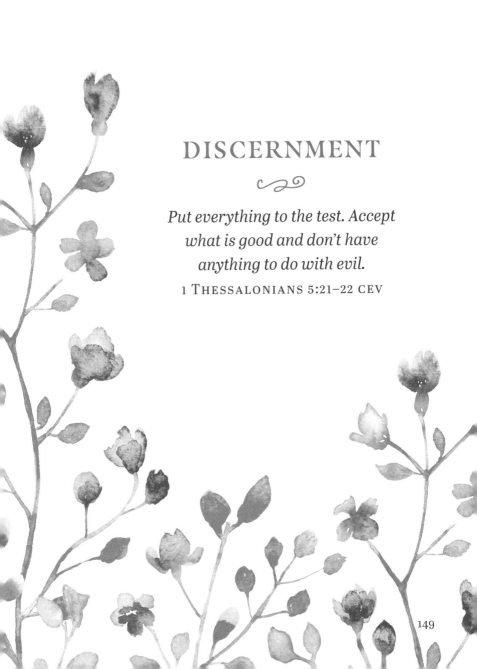

DISCERNMENT

*Put everything to the test. Accept
what is good and don't have
anything to do with evil.*

1 THESSALONIANS 5:21–22 CEV

149

Discernment is more than deciding what it is right and wrong. It is thinking biblically about every aspect of your life and deciding what God wants you to do.

False teaching leads Christians astray. It stands on faulty principles, such as it is best to get a divorce if you and your spouse have fallen out of love or it is okay to swear and tell an occasional dirty joke. False teaching allows authority over God's Word. It says, "It is God's will that you move on when your love has grown cold," or "God has better things to do than worry about a swear word or off-color joke."

The Bible is the only guide to discerning right and wrong from God's point of view. Read it, and learn God's truth. Then, you will be able to recognize false teaching and choose what you know pleases God.

Write God's Word on Your Heart Today

The More You Know is a series of fifteen-second public service announcements presented on television by celebrities. Perhaps you have seen them mixed in with commercials. They remind viewers of simple but important truths, like parents should be involved with their children's education, and exercise is essential to good health.

The more you know, the better you will do in life. And that's why scripture memory is so important—it writes *God's* truths on your heart. The more you know about scripture, the better prepared you are to discern God's will.

Take this quiz. Which of these proverbs is not found in the Bible?

A word fitly spoken is like apples of gold in settings of silver.

God helps those that help themselves.

A bear robbed of her cubs is far less dangerous than a stubborn fool.

If you chose "God helps those that help themselves," you are correct. Benjamin Franklin said that!

When memorizing scripture, be sure to get the words right. Twisting them, even a little, can turn God's truth into a false truth.

Memorize the following:

> *Dear friends, don't believe everyone who claims to have the Spirit of God. Test them all to find out if they really do come from God. Many false prophets have already gone out into the world.*
>
> 1 JOHN 4:1 CEV

> *We must stop acting like children. We must not let deceitful people trick us by their false teachings, which are like winds that toss us around from place to place.*
>
> EPHESIANS 4:14 CEV

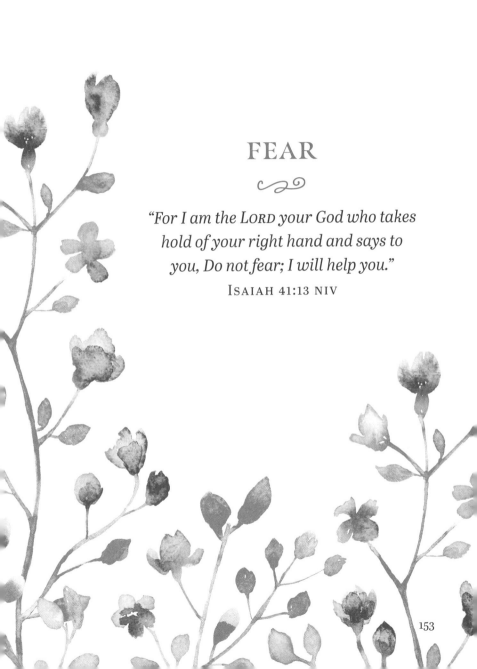

FEAR

*"For I am the L*ORD *your God who takes hold of your right hand and says to you, Do not fear; I will help you."*

ISAIAH 41:13 NIV

Julie thought she did the right thing to help her son, Harper, with his fear of the dark. She read him Mercer Mayer's children's book *There's a Nightmare in My Closet*. In the story, a little boy discovers that the nightmare in his closet, a friendly, silly-looking monster, is more afraid of him than he is of it.

But sometimes, good intentions go awry. Harper did not like the friendly monster. He became even more afraid to go to bed. Every night he climbed into Julie's bed, and after comforting him, she gently took his hand and led him back to his room.

Maybe you have a nightmare in your closet, something that makes you afraid and keeps you awake at night. Turn to God. Allow Him to comfort you. He will take your hand and lead you to a good night's sleep.

Write God's Word on Your Heart Today

Fear is a powerful emotion. Sometimes, as it was with little Harper, people imagine evil that lurks in the unknown, what is not proven, what they cannot see. They lie awake at night dwelling on fear attached to all the "what-ifs." They fear losing their jobs, health, families, and even their lives. Most of the time these fears are perceived and unnecessary, and few are real.

Whatever makes you afraid, you know that you can rely on God to help you. He can handle a crisis, great or small, and He will protect you.

Add these words to those already written on your heart. Memorize them and keep them ready for whenever you feel afraid.

The Lord is my light and my salvation—
whom shall I fear? The Lord is the stronghold
of my life—of whom shall I be afraid?
PSALM 27:1 NIV

God is our refuge and strength, an ever-present help in trouble. Therefore we will not fear, though the earth give way and the mountains fall into the heart of the sea, though its waters roar and foam and the mountains quake with their surging.

PSALM 46:1–3 NIV

You came near when I called to you; you said, "Don't be afraid."

LAMENTATIONS 3:57 NCV

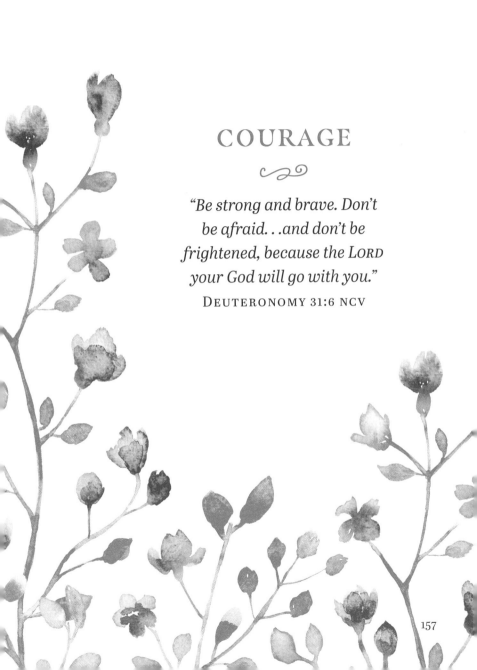

COURAGE

"Be strong and brave. Don't be afraid. . .and don't be frightened, because the LORD your God will go with you."

DEUTERONOMY 31:6 NCV

Amber and her boyfriend, Eric, were in his car heading to what Eric said was "a surprise." Amber could not believe what she saw when they reached his destination: a colorful hot-air balloon, all puffed up and ready to go.

What Eric didn't know was that while Amber was fine in an airplane or looking out the windows of a tall building, the idea of being up high in wide open spaces terrified her. Eric beamed, and Amber prayed silently as she climbed into the balloon's basket: *Yea, though I walk through the valley of the shadow of death, I will fear no evil: for Thou art with me.*

Amber understood that when she was afraid, she could count on God for courage. She also discovered that she liked riding in a hot-air balloon—especially when Eric got down on one knee and said, "Honey, will you marry me?"

Write God's Word on Your Heart Today

If you read the Bible from cover to cover, you will find stories of courage in almost every book. When God's people faced trouble and challenges, He gave them courage. Think about young David standing up to the giant, Goliath. No one thought that this boy had even a chance to prevail over the huge enemy soldier, but he did! David stepped forward with faith, and God provided him the courage and skill to conquer the giant with a single blow.

God will give you courage too. With scripture and faith, you can defeat anything that stands in your way. Reread what Paul says in Ephesians 6:10–18 about putting on the armor of God. Remembering what Paul says will help give you courage.

Bible memory verses become like stones in David's slingshot. When the enemy challenges you, sling scripture at him. It works every time.

Memorize these verses:

"I promise you what I promised Moses: 'Wherever you set foot, you will be on land I have given you. . . .' No one will be able to stand against you as long as you live. For I will be with you as I was with Moses. I will not fail you or abandon you. Be strong and courageous."
JOSHUA 1:3, 5–6 NLT

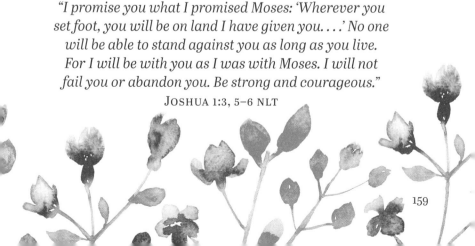

For He Himself has said, "I will never leave you nor forsake you." So we may boldly say: "The LORD is my helper; I will not fear. What can man do to me?"

HEBREWS 13:5–6 NKJV

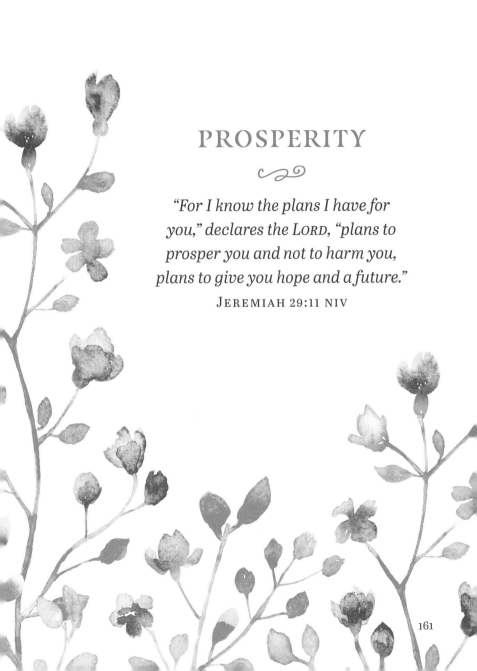

PROSPERITY

"For I know the plans I have for you," declares the Lord, "plans to prosper you and not to harm you, plans to give you hope and a future."

JEREMIAH 29:11 NIV

God promises to prosper you, to make you successful. But sometimes His answers to prayer leave you feeling less than prosperous. What then?

God expects His children to have faith in Him *always.* When they put their faith and trust in Him, they know that He carefully weighs what they ask for in prayer. God might not always give them what they want, but He gives them what He knows is best, and sometimes His best is beyond their understanding.

You are God's beloved child. However He prospers you here on earth, you have hope through Jesus Christ that your future with Him in heaven will prosper you in ways that you cannot begin to imagine. Trust in God's plans for you. Expect prosperity!

Write God's Word on Your Heart Today

What you expect from yourself might differ from what God expects from you. If you set goals without consulting Him, if you run on ahead of God, then prosperity might pass you by. This is why it is important to trust God to help you move forward one step at a time in accordance with His plan.

Some people are not successful at memorizing scripture. Maybe you are one of them. You know that God expects you to commit His Word to memory, but when you try, you become frustrated. Have you asked God to help you? He has a scripture memory plan for everyone.

It might help you to listen to the verse and repeat its words. There are several online Bible sources that will read the Bible aloud to you. BibleGateway.com is one of them.

You might find it effective to memorize scripture by reciting it as if you were acting in a play. Say it aloud as you would in a performance. Practice scripture verses as if they were your lines.

There are many different ways to memorize God's Word. If you get stuck, pray and ask God to align your scripture-memory expectations with His.

Try memorizing these verses:

A faithful person will be richly blessed, but one eager to get rich will not go unpunished.

PROVERBS 28:20 NIV

"If they obey and serve [God], they will spend the rest of their days in prosperity and their years in contentment."

JOB 36:11 NIV

DISTRACTIONS

*Be alert and of sober mind. Your enemy
the devil prowls around like a roaring
lion looking for someone to devour.*

1 Peter 5:8 niv

Imagine living in Jesus' time. Even the busiest marketplace back then cannot compare to the distractions that we face today. In Jesus' time, it was easy to get away from all the noise and activity and focus only on God.

Today's world is fast paced and overflowing with diversions— cell phones, computers, video games, television, errands, and daily tasks. The more distracted we become, the less focused we can be on God. And Satan likes it that way. His goal is to take over the world by getting us to focus on him instead of our heavenly Father.

So all day, every day, practice keeping your mind fixed on God. Pay attention to the words of 1 Peter 5:8: "Be alert."

The enemy is everywhere flinging distractions at you and always inventing new ones. Get him out of your way.

Write God's Word on Your Heart Today

Whenever you read the Bible or try to memorize scripture, Satan will try to distract you; the telephone rings, your child needs something, or your mind turns to things you need to do. Satan hates it when you fill your heart with God's Word. Knowing scripture and including it in your daily life is a powerful tool against evil. Satan has no power over the Word of God.

Self-discipline and commitment are necessary for scripture memorization. If you are easily distracted, try these tips:

1. Think ahead and try to distance yourself from any distractions.
2. Set aside a specific time each day to memorize scripture. Choose a time when you're least distracted.
3. Turn off your phone, TV, computer, and other devices that might distract you.
4. Tell your family that you need some quiet time to memorize scripture. Better yet, make scripture memory time family time.
5. Recognize the importance of memorizing scripture and make it a priority.

Memorize these verses and recall them whenever you feel distracted:

My dear children, you belong to God and have defeated them; because God's Spirit, who is in you, is greater than the devil, who is in the world.

1 JOHN 4:4 NCV

Submit yourselves, then, to God. Resist the devil, and he will flee from you.

JAMES 4:7 NIV

"Get out of here, Satan," Jesus told him. "For the Scriptures say, 'You must worship the LORD your God and serve only him.'"

MATTHEW 4:10 NLT

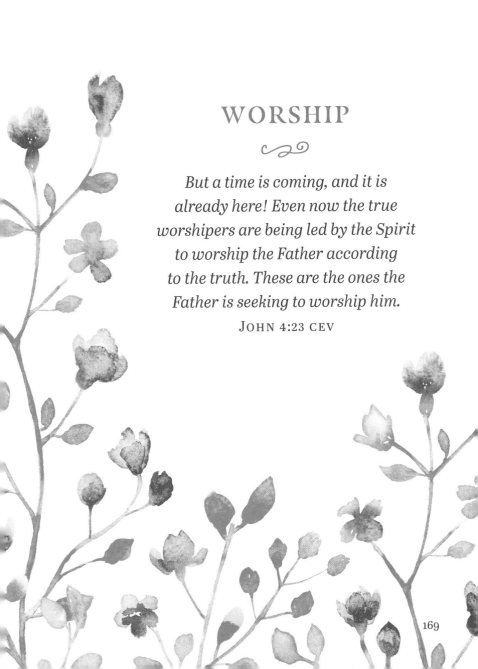

WORSHIP

*But a time is coming, and it is
already here! Even now the true
worshipers are being led by the Spirit
to worship the Father according
to the truth. These are the ones the
Father is seeking to worship him.*

JOHN 4:23 CEV

When asked by her Sunday school teacher, "What is worship?" Kelli answered, "It's going to church on Sunday and spending an hour with God." Sadly, that is how some adults define worship too.

True worship is a twenty-four-hour event every day. It is making God your first priority and honoring Him by living a holy lifestyle. Worshipping God in the Spirit means worshipping God always in your heart and soul, not just in church on Sunday. Worshipping Him in truth means worshipping Him as the one and only God as described in the Bible and not a god made up of false doctrine.

A great reward comes when you worship God in the Spirit and in truth. He fills up your heart with His love.

Write God's Word on Your Heart Today

Memorizing scripture is an important way to worship God. Memorizing His Word gives you a greater understanding of Him. The more you understand about God, the more able you are to worship Him in the Spirit and in truth. Memorizing scripture also gives you insight into your own life and God's plans for you. When you memorize from the New Testament, especially the words of Jesus, you learn to imitate Christ in your daily living. Imitating Jesus helps create a holy lifestyle, which is another way to honor and worship Him. The goal for any true worshipper of God is to make anything he or she does an act of worship—an act pleasing to God.

Psalm 119 (CEV) has several things to say about the importance of knowing God's Word: "I treasure your word above all else; it keeps me from sinning against you" (v. 11). "Your word is a lamp that gives light wherever I walk" (v. 105). "Understanding your word brings light to the minds of ordinary people" (v. 130).

Honor God today and worship Him by memorizing His Word:

We should be grateful that we were given a kingdom that cannot be shaken. And in this kingdom we please God by worshiping him and by showing him great honor and respect.

HEBREWS 12:28 CEV

"Fear God and give him glory, because the hour of his judgment has come. Worship him who made the heavens, the earth, the sea and the springs of water."

REVELATION 14:7 NIV

HUMILITY

*The wise woman builds her
house, but with her own hands
the foolish one tears hers down.*

PROVERBS 14:1 NIV

Elaine took great pride in her decorating skills, especially at Christmastime. She held several parties during the season so friends and acquaintances could see her lovely Christmas tree and sample her delicious cookies and appetizers.

Noticing her husband's business partner admiring the tree, Elaine asked, "Don't you just love it?"

"It's nice," he answered, "but it's so perfect that I'm afraid to touch it."

Sometimes pride in our works gets in the way of the warmth of humility. Most visitors to Elaine's home would have agreed that it was beautiful but cold. It lacked the welcoming friend-liness that comes with a humble heart.

In his book *Humility*, Andrew Murray wrote, "Pride must die in you, or nothing of heaven can live in you." If Elaine had believed this and put it into practice, the light of Christ would have filled her home with a beauty unrivaled by her perfect food and decorations.

Write God's Word on Your Heart Today

A few Christians allow pride to get in the way of memorizing scripture. "I know what's in the Bible," they say. "I've read the whole thing, so why do I need to memorize it?" Some feel important because they know what is in the Bible. The Pharisees in Jesus' time were similar. They considered themselves so devoted to God and the laws of scripture that they were blind to the fact that Jesus was the Messiah, God's Chosen One, His Son. They stood on street corners praying to God, and yet they did everything in their power to stop Jesus.

Thinking that you know what is in the Bible leaves you blind to the truth of God's Word. As you read scripture and recall it from memory, God enlightens its meaning for you personally.

Jesus is the best example of one who memorized scripture. He used scripture throughout His ministry to teach and also to rebuke. If He, the Son of God, needed to memorize scripture, then how can any Christian be exempt?

Pray and ask God to forgive you for times when you have been less than humble. Ask Him to lead you away from pride and toward humility. Then, memorize these verses:

"For I tell you that unless your righteousness surpasses that of the Pharisees and the teachers of the law, you will certainly not enter the kingdom of heaven."

MATTHEW 5:20 NIV

He guides the humble in what is right and teaches them his way.

PSALM 25:9 NIV

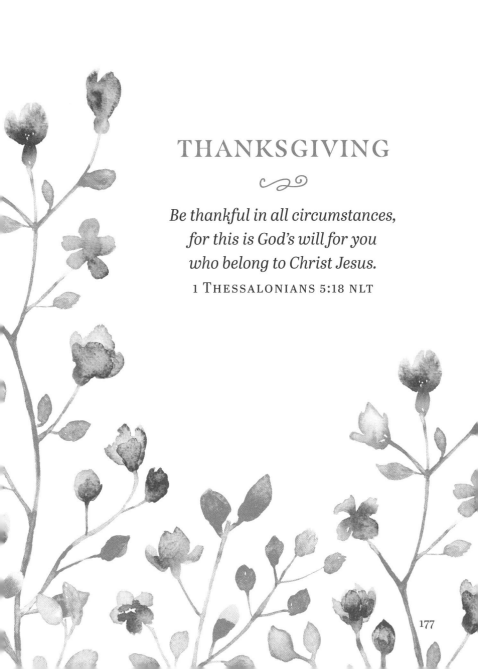

THANKSGIVING

*Be thankful in all circumstances,
for this is God's will for you
who belong to Christ Jesus.*

1 THESSALONIANS 5:18 NLT

When Paul was imprisoned in Rome, he wrote to his fellow Christians, "Sing and make music from your heart to the Lord, always giving thanks to God the Father for everything, in the name of our Lord Jesus Christ" (Ephesians 5:19–20 NIV). Focus on that word *always*. Paul was telling his friends that they should remember God's blessings always, no matter what.

In his letter to the Thessalonians, Paul told his friends to be thankful in all circumstances. The focus word here is *in*. Paul did not say to be thankful *for* all circumstances but *in* them.

When you find yourself in difficult circumstances, remember to always give thanks to God for being with you. Thank Him for His blessings and His never-ending love for you. In all circumstances He will help you. God will see you through.

Write God's Word on Your Heart Today

"It was the best of times, it was the worst of times, it was the age of wisdom, it was the age of foolishness, it was the epoch of belief, it was the epoch of incredulity, it was the season of Light, it was the season of Darkness, it was the spring of hope, it was the winter of despair, we had everything before us, we had nothing before us."

These words from Charles Dickens' novel, *A Tale of Two Cities*, describe life. It is a journey of widespread opposites, the best of times and the worst of times. It is easy to thank God in the best of times and difficult to thank Him in the worst. Still, this is what He wants us to do, and memorizing scripture is one way to guarantee that we have the words to thank Him when our own words fail.

Do an Internet search of scripture songs, and you will find many. Learn some of them, and sing to the Lord. Also, read 2 Samuel 22. Memorize these words David spoke in his song of praise:

"The Lord lives!
Blessed be my Rock!
Let God be exalted,
The Rock of my salvation!
It is God who avenges me,
And subdues the peoples under me;
He delivers me from my enemies. . . .
Therefore I will give thanks to You, O Lord. . .
And sing praises to Your name."

2 Samuel 22:47–50 NKJV

CREATION

Everything on earth, shout with joy to God! Sing about his glory! Make his praise glorious! Say to God, "Your works are amazing!"

PSALM 66:1–3 NCV

The Metropolitan Museum of Art is filled with creative works in many styles using many different mediums. If you wander through its collections, something will catch your eye. You will think, or say out loud, "Isn't that beautiful!"

Your idea of beauty may differ from someone else's. We see beauty through our God-given perceptions, and beauty is, as the old saying goes, in the eye of the beholder.

God, the Creator, has made for us a beautiful world. Some of His beautiful creation is outwardly apparent—the Grand Canyon, a quiet moonlit night, soft snow resting on stiff, winter-worn branches—and some is hidden, just waiting for us to find it.

The French painter Camille Pissarro said, "Blessed are they who see beautiful things in humble places where other people see nothing." Look around today for the hidden beauty in God's creation, and be blessed by what you find.

Write God's Word on Your Heart Today

[Jesus] said to them, 'Go into all the world and preach the gospel to all creation' " (Mark 16:15 NIV). If you are a follower of Jesus Christ, then you are His disciple, and His command to preach the gospel to all creation is meant for you.

There are many different ways to share God's Word. Preachers preach it from the pulpit. Singers sing about it, and writers write about it. God bestows on His children the gift of creativity so they can share Him with others. Like Him, we are creators, but on a much smaller scale. Our creativity is limited by what our bodies can do and what our human minds are capable of understanding.

In what creative ways can you share the gospel with your community? Some women embroider scripture verses onto blankets to give to the homeless. Others create scripture banners for their churches. Making scripture key chains and jewelry, putting scripture verses on T-shirts, and visiting nursing homes to sing scripture songs are other ways to reach out.

Decide on a creative way to share a scripture verse or passage with a person or group in your community. Focus on the meaning of the passage and its words.

One of the best memory verses to share is this:

For God so loved the world that he gave his one and only Son, that whoever believes in him shall not perish but have eternal life.

JOHN 3:16 NIV

ETERNAL LIFE

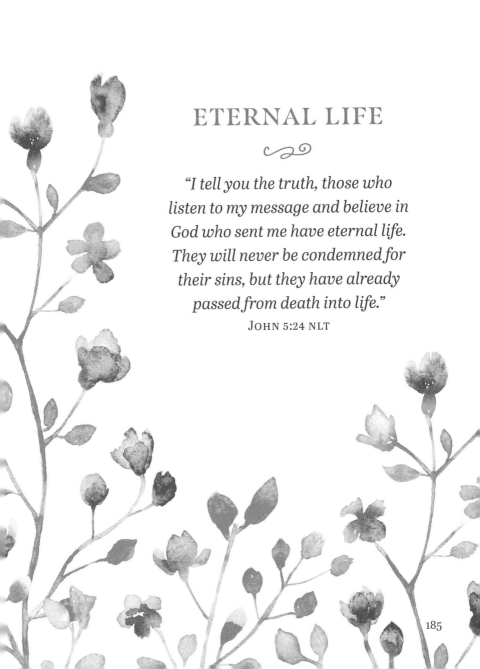

*"I tell you the truth, those who
listen to my message and believe in
God who sent me have eternal life.
They will never be condemned for
their sins, but they have already
passed from death into life."*

JOHN 5:24 NLT

The nineteenth-century poet Henry Van Dyke wrote that passing from death into eternal life is like a ship sailing over the horizon. We see our loved one off at the shore. Then we watch until her ship is a tiny dot on the horizon, and when she disappears from sight, someone says, "There she goes!" And just at that moment, there are other eyes watching her coming over the horizon and other voices ready to take up the glad shout, "Here she comes!"

God promises eternal life to those who believe that Jesus paid the price for their sins. For believers, death is not forever. They are parted for just a little while until a voice on the other side shouts, "Here she comes!"

Write God's Word on Your Heart Today

Do you struggle with knowing what to say at a funeral or what to write inside a sympathy card? Although death has come to every human since the beginning of time, many people still wonder what to say.

The God of all comfort (2 Corinthians 1:3) understands that death causes pain for the living. And because He provides for *all* our needs, He provides through His scripture comforting words and counsel to ease the pain.

It is most comforting knowing that heaven is real. God treated John to a glimpse of heaven, and John wrote about it in Revelation 21:10–27. If you haven't done so, read these verses in your Bible.

The living also find comfort knowing that their way to heaven is by God's grace through Christ Jesus. Separation from their deceased Christian family and friends is only temporary because God's gift of salvation guarantees eternal life.

There are a number of scripture verses appropriate for the death of a loved one. Hide these in your heart so you will be ready when you need them:

*Precious in the sight of the Lord is the
death of his faithful servants.*

PSALM 116:15 NIV

*Good people pass away; the godly often die before
their time. But no one seems to care or wonder why.
No one seems to understand that God is protecting
them from the evil to come. For those who follow
godly paths will rest in peace when they die.*

ISAIAH 57:1–2 NLT

GOD'S PERFECT LOVE

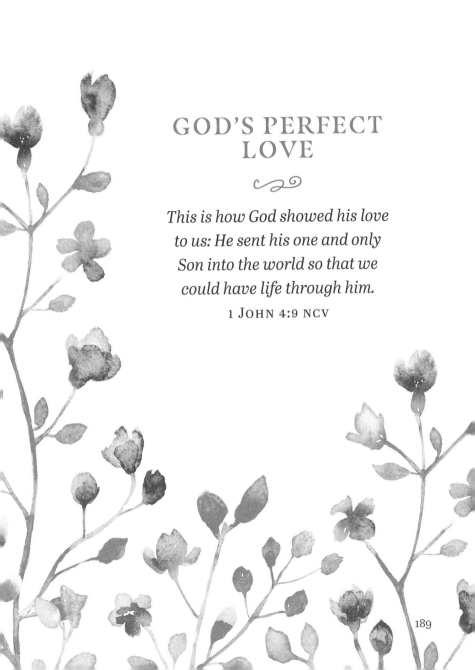

This is how God showed his love to us: He sent his one and only Son into the world so that we could have life through him.

1 JOHN 4:9 NCV

What parents wouldn't give their lives to save their child? This is true love—loving someone so deeply that you will do anything to keep him or her from harm. This is the sort of love that imitates God's love.

God created us to be His children. He is our Father, perfect in every way. When God saw that His children could not resist sin, He made a plan to save them. He sent His only Son, His beloved Son, to be punished for the sins of His children. God sent Jesus to suffer and die so that His children could live forever with Him in His heaven, gloriously alive, happy, and free from sin!

You can't begin to understand how much God loves you. His love for you is the purest, forever love, and best of all—perfect.

Write God's Word on Your Heart Today

Memorizing scripture and spending time in the Word of God creates a close bond between you and your heavenly Father. God's love is unconditional. His will for you and all of His children is to accept Christ's gift of salvation so you can experience the fullness of His love. When you open up your heart to God, He pours His love into it. He creates in you a bottomless heart that can never get enough of His perfect love.

Meditate on His love for you. Listen to worship songs, let God fill you up with love, and know that the love you feel now, in your earthly body, is just a portion of the love waiting for you in heaven.

Memorize these verses about God's love using some of the tips you have learned in this book. Write them on your heart, and think of them every day.

For I am convinced that neither death nor life, neither angels nor demons, neither the present nor the future, nor any powers, neither height nor depth, nor anything else in all creation, will be able to separate us from the love of God that is in Christ Jesus our Lord.

ROMANS 8:38–39 NIV

"The LORD your God is in your midst, a mighty one who will save; he will rejoice over you with gladness; he will quiet you by his love; he will exult over you with loud singing."

ZEPHANIAH 3:17 ESV